T0354994

I AM NOT YOUR
BOY

I AM NOT YOUR
BOY

RONEK PATEL

ARCHWAY
PUBLISHING

Archway Publishing books may be ordered through booksellers or by contacting:

Archway Publishing
1663 Liberty Drive
Bloomington, IN 47403
www.archwaypublishing.com
844-669-3957

ISBN: 978-1-6657-7205-1 (sc)
ISBN: 978-1-6657-7207-5 (hc)
ISBN: 978-1-6657-7206-8 (e)

Library of Congress Control Number: 2025901142

Print information available on the last page.

Archway Publishing rev. date: 01/25/2025

CONTENTS

MY STORY

Have you ever felt discarded like a piece of trash? Just feeling like you're at the bottom of the garbage bin, looking up and wondering if you'll ever feel accepted? Perhaps you're in a place where your dreams seem utterly unachievable, and the struggle to rise from the depths seems insurmountable, your worth concealed beneath layers of doubt.

Growing Up

I didn't always feel that way growing up. Maybe it was simmering beneath the surface all along. With three older sisters and a single mom who divorced my dad when I was in the fourth grade due to his affair, life was far from simple. My mom raised us on just $20,000 a year, working tirelessly to make sure we had a decent life. My bond with my dad was weak; he was always wrestling with his own problems. But my mom was my anchor, pushing herself day and night for our sake. I was the only one in my family born in the States; my sisters and parents all came from India. My mom was determined to ensure we wouldn't face the hardships she did when immigrating and establishing herself here. She emphasized financial independence above all else and pushed us to succeed and blend in smoothly with others.

It seemed to be a typical aspect of Indian culture: striving for success and constantly being mindful of how others perceive you. The common Indian phrase, "what will people think?" significantly influenced how I live my life, constantly seeking validation and finding it difficult to be vulnerable. I didn't get validation from my dad, so I constantly sought it from others. His lack of loyalty made monogamy crucial for me. My mother allowed me a lot of independence, making me search for caretakers later in life. She also stayed single intentionally ever since their divorce, so I struggled to understand or closely experience a stable relationship.

My childhood wasn't terrible. It definitely could have been worse. But it did shape how I became an adult, requiring a lot of deep searching to understand its impact on my ability to navigate potential obstacles in my life.

College

When I decided to go to college out of state, it was because I wanted to experience life beyond the familiar confines of my hometown. At that time, I had a girlfriend, but our relationship was on shaky ground. Moving away only added more strain to an already fragile connection, making the challenge of maintaining a long-distance relationship even harder. We never had a proper conversation about ending things; we just slowly drifted apart, avoiding the glaring issues between us. Adding to my confusion was my struggle with understanding my sexuality. I didn't know if I was gay, straight, or bi, finding myself drawn to both men and women. College felt like the perfect place to explore these feelings, far from the watchful eyes of familiar faces. It was an opportunity to reinvent myself and discover who I really was.

I longed for a meaningful relationship but didn't know how to find one. My first semester was a whirlwind of spontaneity—I met new friends, attended parties, and had casual flings. While I was eager to explore my sexuality, the college I attended didn't have a large gay community. The few gay men around were older locals, not students, and were usually married or already in committed relationships. It was tough to navigate this part of my identity within such limitations.

Choosing a major was another struggle. To be honest, I was surprised when I got accepted into the university because I wasn't exactly a standout student in high school. My lack of academic motivation came from not having any big dreams or a clear vision for my future. I wanted to be successful but had no clue how to get there. This lack of direction left me feeling unmotivated, as if I were merely existing rather than truly living.

HIV

I came home for Christmas break from college and was turning 19 on New Year's Eve. It's the best birthday, everyone celebrates it. Right beforehand, I got incredibly sick. I ended up in the hospital with severe nausea, vomiting, and diarrhea. At this point I could count on one hand how many people I had sex with but just to make sure, I asked the hospital to run an STD test. I wasn't practicing safe sex, and neither were my friends. I know those symptoms didn't exactly call for an STD test, but I was paranoid and wanted to make sure.

It turns out the test came back negative, and it was diagnosed as a simple bacterial infection. I took the medication and got better just in time for my 19th birthday party, which my best friend was hosting for me. I had a blast, but I still didn't feel confident that the hospital had really checked thoroughly. After my birthday, I borrowed my mom's car. I told her I left something at the party, but I actually drove to the local Planned Parenthood. I needed to make sure I was clear of STDs.

The testing at Planned Parenthood was enough to relieve my worries. I went back to school the following week. I was back to normal and feeling good. I still didn't know what to major in or whether I was straight, gay, or bi, but at least I got over the stomach bug and got to see some friends from home. Then I got a call from Planned Parenthood. I thought perhaps I had forgotten something there, so I answered while on my way to an internship. They ended up telling me over the phone that I was HIV positive, and I completely froze.

All these thoughts flooded my mind at once. How do I break the news to the people I've been intimate with? Did I inadvertently put anyone at risk? Will I be able to live a long, healthy life? How do I get the care I need while I'm still in school? Should I confide in my friends and family? In the end, I decided to call everyone I'd been with and advised them to get tested. They were understandably angry, but I had just found out myself and wanted to ensure they were safe. Thankfully, they all reported negative results, which brought me some relief, but it left me wondering—who did I get this from?

To this day, that question remains unanswered. That's when I began to pressure myself to figure out the direction of my life. I realized I needed clarity and focus. I started by choosing my major and opted for Psychology. I also made the difficult decision to embrace my identity as a gay man, reasoning that women might not want to be with someone who has HIV, whereas in the gay community, it seemed somewhat more accepted. I resolved to keep this part of my life private, only disclosing it if I was going to be intimate with someone. I decided to carry this burden alone, without telling my friends at school or my family.

Throughout my entire college experience, I quietly bore the weight of constant rejection. Each time I shared my status with a man, hoping for love or even just a connection, I was cast aside, disregarded like trash. Age made no difference—young or old, their reactions left me feeling worthless. I kept my emotional turmoil hidden, fearing the need to explain my status and the relentless rejections. Financial struggles pushed me to graduate a year early, saving a year's worth of tuition. Immersing myself in schoolwork and internships became my escape from the distressing chaos of my love life. Though I tried to be consistent at the gym, the motivation often waned. After all, what was the point of looking good if, in the end, I would only be discarded?

Back in 2011, the stigma surrounding HIV wasn't as intense as it was in the '80s, but it wasn't as progressive as it is today. We didn't really understand the long-term effects of the medications or the actual risk of infection when using them. People my age were terrified. Older generations knew more but were still deeply scared, likely having lost friends to the disease. Despite it all, I still needed love and acceptance. I also found myself growing angrier at friends who casually mentioned their unprotected one-night stands—they couldn't fathom why I was so upset. I still wasn't telling people, so I just left them confused.

During my senior year, I couldn't take the isolation any longer.

Frustrated and feeling utterly alone, I took a bold step and created a video revealing my HIV status, sharing it with everyone on my social media. The reaction was immediate; it spread across campus overnight. The next day, as I went to class, people approached me, expressing their genuine concern and telling me they had no idea. For the first time, I started to feel accepted and cared for, even by people I barely knew.

Becoming More Open

Suddenly, it dawned on me. When I open up and share who I am, I attract acceptance and support. In hiding, I faced a harsh, unfiltered world where I felt constantly under attack. But by sharing myself, I found that most of the people around me were lifting me up, understanding me without need for explanation. Since that realization, I've embraced openness about every aspect of my life, allowing the world to see the real me. This approach not only welcomed those who accepted me but also made it easier to distance myself from those who didn't belong in my life.

This revelation drove me to share it with as many people as possible. I launched a public speaking business, eager to disseminate my message to the world. I hoped that by opening up about my own vulnerabilities, others could learn and protect themselves sooner. I was 22 and fearless. However, entering the corporate world presented a challenge. I felt I couldn't be my genuine self anymore because everything was so rigid and conformist. To be seen and respected, you had to fit a certain mold. Success seemed to demand a certain behavior. This pressure made it hard for me to be authentic, and it took years before I managed to bring my true self to work every day and feel good about it.

I took it upon myself to launch several LGBTQ initiatives within companies that hadn't placed much emphasis on the matter. I pitched my ideas to key decision-makers in various organizations, urging them to prioritize this often-overlooked issue. It wasn't part of my primary job responsibilities, but I was driven by a deep desire to protect others and give a voice to those who felt unheard. With each success, people began to notice my genuine passion and empathy shining through. I was determined to ensure that no one would ever have to experience the same sense of isolation that I once did.

Relationships

When I graduated college, I was in a long-term relationship with a man who was 35 years older than me. I felt happy and accepted. Our relationship lasted five years, during which I began to realize I was stuck in the same patterns. I kept my HIV status a secret in college, hoping for acceptance. In the corporate world, I conformed and stayed silent to fit their expectations. Even in my relationship, I was living his life rather than my own. I constantly sought to meet others' expectations instead of expressing my true self, all for the sake of acceptance, despite my vocal involvement in various public initiatives.

After that breakup, I went on a journey of self-discovery through various dating experiences. I spent time with older men, peers my age, and occasionally engaged in casual encounters. I dipped my toes into the world of dating apps and even tried out some unconventional relationships. I also gave dating women another shot. It felt like I was just going along with anyone who showed interest in me, rather than truly figuring out what I wanted for myself. My relationships were going nowhere. People kept advising me to be casual and just go with the flow, but that wasn't fulfilling my long-term needs. I had to face some hard truths with myself and those around me. After making a firm decision on what I truly wanted in the long run, I got better at expressing my true intentions. I set clear boundaries for those whose intentions didn't match mine. It was incredibly uncomfortable to turn away people who seemed great, but it was crucial for protecting my future goals and myself.

Weekly therapy sessions became a constant in my life for years, helping me understand how to build the strongest connections and find what truly suited me. I opened myself up and drew back the curtains to my soul, facing profound heartache and extraordinary love. Every experience, every trial and error, has led me to write this book.

INTRODUCTION

"I Am Not Your Boy" is a self-help book that educates young adults on navigating relationships with older adults. It highlights the insights and life lessons that lead to informed personal choices, while addressing the dangers of being exploited, manipulated, and losing control over one's destiny. This guide confronts the stigma associated with age differences, provides ways to identify predator tendencies, and toxic "situationships," discusses hookup culture, explores the origins of certain kinks and fetishes. Additionally, it offers advice on how to extricate oneself from parental dependencies and find autonomy, empowering the reader to achieve control, authority, self-identity, and the means to forge stronger connections with themselves and others. "I Am Not Your Boy" equips you to build an authentic self, empowering you to step into the world with confidence, aware of what to avoid and what to pursue.

At 32 years of age, Ronek Patel recounts his interactions with older adults. Over the course of several years of therapy sessions—he began at 19 when he was diagnosed with HIV, transmitted to him by an older person—and being the most junior member in nearly all professional settings, he has striven to be acknowledged at the same level as his elder colleagues. Ronek's distinctive journey serves as an inspiration to young adults, encouraging them to recognize signs of dominance and to position themselves assertively when engaging with those who might assert their superiority based on their age and presumed wisdom.

At present, the subject at hand is not a common topic of mainstream conversations. Our society is grappling with a myriad of problems, and while it is not feasible to address every single one, there remains a significant oversight in the conversation concerning the use of the word 'boy' in romantic relationships. The term is recognized as having racist connotations due to its historical employment by slave owners to demean the males they enslaved. However, its pejorative connotations within the dynamic of relationships have not been widely acknowledged by society. While this book does not specifically address matters of race and ethnicity, it's important to note that the word 'boy' crops up in both realms.

The term 'boy' may appear innocuous but is imbued with a subtle undertone of belittlement that warrants careful consideration in its use throughout various forms of human interaction. In the delicate balance of relationships, its improper use can covertly, but decidedly, alter the distribution of power. Detached from the disgrace associated with racial disparagement, its commonplace employment within romantic contexts has escaped the critical examination it deserves. How can we, as a responsible society, overlook the use of this term, intended to diminish, as it is repurposed without contention, reducing adults to a lesser stature?

In professional settings, referring to a woman as 'girl' is correctly met with allegations of sexism—so why doesn't the analogous act of referring to an adult man as 'boy' provoke a comparable uproar? In the gay community, 'boy' has become an ingrained part of the dialogue, yet its constant repetition does not incite the collective consciousness to recognize the widespread belittlement it conveys. When you're in the straight world, you hear 'boy' tossed around in a way that kinda pushes grown men back to their kid days, though it's not as common as it is with gay folks.

Diving into these pages will, I hope, shed light on what one goes through when being stamped with the label 'boy' whether you are straight, gay, or bisexual, and how it nudges the course we take in life.

We should not tolerate being relegated, demeaned, or sidelined by those who believe they can devalue us merely by using the term 'boy' without facing the acrid rebuke of their offense.

This issue transcends mere emotional injury—it results in the erosion of our authority, our independence, and forces us back into a state of repressed juvenile silence. The word carries with it an odious implication of domination, stripping us of control over our futures, and yet, it manages to sneak past our defenses unchallenged. It is imperative that we put a stop to this folly and claim the respect that is rightfully ours.

I am not a therapist, nor do I have life fully figured out. Much like you, I am a young man. The label 'boy' has frequently been ascribed to me, and societal norms dismiss its significance as inconsequential. My life journey has been accompanied by persistent adversity. At nineteen, I was diagnosed with HIV. As someone of Indian heritage, I have faced racism within the predominantly white culture of America. Additionally, our young people are often dismissed into this 'boy' category, depreciating our value and obstructing our recognition as equal members of society. My experiences have been varied, encompassing challenges you may resonate with or wish to avoid—including emotionally abusive relationships, unhealthy situationships, paternal disapproval, body image issues, and the burdensome expectations imposed by family, work, and the greater society.

I wrote this book after witnessing and enduring the effects of generational behaviors on us young individuals. Such societal pressures can lead to substance misuse, mistrust, an inability to be vulnerable, and clinging to erroneous beliefs, all of which can impede the development of a strong sense of self and hinder the ability to forge strong relationships and connections with others.

Though I acknowledge my own imperfections and continue to wade through the complexities of life, I have come to understand the importance of self-care for mental well-being. If we are unable to protect our own welfare, is it wise to allow others to dictate our life paths? This book aims to be a navigational tool through the rugged terrain of life, providing approaches to defend yourself and secure your future, helping you to cultivate only the strongest relationships and connections in your life while helping to promote a high self-worth.

PAIN POINT

WHAT IS SEEMINGLY INNOCENT, CAN TURN YOUR WHOLE
WORLD AROUND.

Love, fills us with a rush of dopamine and lifts our serotonin levels,
becoming an addictive source of joy. It envelops our hearts in a deep,
passionate embrace, a gentle affection that weaves itself into every corner
of our existence. It guides the beat of our thoughts, influencing decisions
and judgments we'd never make with just reason alone.

Fear, perhaps the most potent emotion known to us, can be an
overwhelming force gripping the very core of our being. It dictates the
rhythm of our thoughts, the depth of our feelings, and the actions we
dare to undertake. We can feel powerless when it overwhelms us and
makes us incredibly scared. This primal sentinel stands guard, a vigilant
protector that guides us through the perils of life, ensuring our survival.
However, it can also lead us into an endless black hole, limiting us to
only feeling scared. Yet, intertwined with this formidable feeling is the
necessity of its existence—for within its embrace, we find the strength
to love, the courage to embrace life, and the hope to flourish amidst all
the temptations out there.

What happens when fear is combined with the emotion of love? The
very notion sends shivers down my spine. Just think about it – merging
two such polar forces, one that swells the heart with its profound and
passionate embrace, the other that chokes the soul with its cold, foreboding grip. The contradiction is as stark as night against day. Love fills us
with a boundless warmth, a tender affection that seeps into every crevice
of our being; fear, in contrast, is a piercing alarm that awakens us to
looming threats and unseen dangers.

Love activates our fears, while fears can, in turn, incite love. We want to love, but our past experiences make us fearful. Our fears protect us from dangers, but sometimes we need to overcome them to become better people and feel more confident in ourselves. Such fears render us bewildered and prompt irrational behavior. Meanwhile, love can engender an insatiable craving, leaving us dependent on the ensuing dopamine surge. This interplay drives us to the brink of madness. Hence, the term "crazy love" is not without basis. Upon developing an attraction to someone, we often find ourselves reacting as if in survival mode. We meet another person, and we latch onto them relentlessly. Surrender is not an option—we feel compelled to mask our fears and surmount them, all for the sake of maintaining attraction to our chosen person. Maybe it's the fear of losing them or the fear of not finding someone else, but we find ourselves caught in this frenzy. It's hard to tell if this is genuine love or if it's an unsettled issue within us. Either way, the crazy love we feel still drives our actions.

Why do we constantly find ourselves having to face our fears just to feel love? The answer is rooted deep within us; love and the companionship it offers are as crucial to our well-being as food and water are to our physical health. We all yearn to love and be loved, but somehow, to achieve this, we must overcome our inner barriers and let love in. The fear we experience is inside us. Without such fears, we could see others more clearly and be more empathetic. Without these fears, we could be better partners and build stronger connections with others. Yet, we often fear losing that exhilarating high, or we're too scared to even pursue it. At times, we approach love with caution, but the reality that we need to experience both fear and love to truly grasp the full spectrum of human emotion is perplexing yet undeniable.

When we let fear and love mix within us, it makes us vulnerable. It's like we're opening a crack in our hearts – it's terrifying, but it's genuine. Take, for instance, meeting someone new and falling in love. This person seems to embody everything you've ever wanted, and they make you feel incredibly special. But something holds you back – the familiarity. It feels like a déjà vu from a past relationship where you got hurt. Now, you're projecting this fear onto the new person, even though they aren't your ex. The moment you decide to give this new relationship a chance, despite the painful memories and the resemblance to your past, you chose to overcome fear to experience love but also open yourself up to vulnerability.

But that's when we step into this space where we can actually connect with others on a level that's deep and true. It's about letting our guard down, about throwing away the masks we wear and just being who we truly are, unapologetically. This raw honesty, it wipes out the shadows of doubt and confusion, making room for us to understand and be understood. It's in that space where we're our true selves that the most beautiful relationships come to life.

With vulnerability, comes risk. There will always be the chance of getting hurt. It also is a chance for connection and growth. It's a gamble. Who we allow ourselves to be vulnerable with can dramatically impact our growth and ability to love. We've all put our vulnerability in the wrong hands. We also put our vulnerability in the right hands and learned how that feels. It's incredible.

When we put our vulnerability in the wrong hands, we lose vision. We lose sanity. We lose ourselves. We can be the most productive, successful person in the world but when it comes to love, fear, and vulnerability, we crumble. What is seemingly innocent, can turn our whole world around. That's why it's imperative to dive into it with all the resources possible. Learning from others and ourselves.

And let's throw in another twist to the mix of fear, love, and vulnerability we already deal with: our age. Older folks sometimes tell us that we haven't lived long enough to grasp love's intricacies. They've endured serious heartache and believed we haven't experienced enough to truly understand who to love or how to express that love properly. Hearing this while we're still finding our way in love can make us doubt if our choices are right or if we really comprehend the risks. What they often miss is the weight of our experiences. We've felt the highs and lows. We know how certain people make us feel and what qualities draw us to particular individuals. We have valuable knowledge that's frequently underrated. With that knowledge comes strength. The more we know, the more powerful we become, equipping us to handle love just as well as our older counterparts.

When we are young and in love, it feels wonderful; however, at times, we bestow our affections too indiscriminately. Sometimes, we devote so much time and energy to people who can't give us what we truly want, resulting in feelings of hurt. We do it because it feels good at the moment, but when we're constantly chasing people who can't fulfill our true desires, we misplace a sense of selfhood and individuality. We transform into someone different, morphing into someone's partner rather than remaining true to ourselves. This shift fosters dependency rather than self-sufficiency. We forsake other passions, such as our friendships, professional pursuits, family ties, hobbies, and interests. Ultimately, it radically alters our life's trajectory.

We end up missing out on things we truly enjoy. We miss out on the perfect opportunity that gives us everything we are looking for. We allow these to slip by because we end up infatuated with someone. Life is so short, yet we convince ourselves we have all the time in the world.

Another way we form a sense of dependency rather than self-sufficiency is when we fill the void left by our parents, searching for another caretaker to play the role that once, or supposed to have, surrounded us with love and security. This transition, laced with vulnerability, entails trusting someone as we did our own family, allowing them to guide and comfort us. It brings a measure of risk, yet also the potential for a deep connection that can restore our sense of wholeness.

We are frequently told that we must focus on self-improvement before we are capable of experiencing love. This is, in fact, a misconception. This antiquated fairytale insisting we have to have our lives perfectly lined up before we can even consider diving into a relationship. It's that tired mantra that we must first adore ourselves to the fullest before we're qualified to give love to another soul. I've got friends who preach self-improvement like gospel before even considering a date, but here's my take—I'm not entirely on board. Sure, self-reflection and growth are key to any fulfilling relationship. But wait around until you're 'perfect'? No way. Loving and being loved is our right. It's this incredible force that shapes us into better versions of ourselves, teaching lessons that just don't come when you're riding solo.

How about we're just a bit more selective about who we let see our soft side? I've been digging deep, trying to understand what our younger self needs to feel whole, to act boldly. It's about knowing what opens us up, letting you lay your guard down without feeling exposed. Taking it slow at the start means we can leapfrog through life, sidestepping the pitfalls of reckless romances. It's about building something real, fast-tracking to our true callings and heart's desires.

You might think it's a piece of cake, but trust me, it's anything but. Over time, we have developed unconventional ways of feeling convenient love. There are so many folks out there now, a whole world brimming over with hearts and minds to meet and getting in touch with them is a snap with apps. It's like the whole world is at our fingertips, an open invitation to explore every nook and cranny. Sometimes I just look up at the stars and feel a bit swamped. There's just so much out there, so many paths to take, and each and every choice feels like a leap.

Often times we find unconventional ways of feeling convenient love. Practices such as hookups, kinks/fetishes, and situationships stray from traditional relationship norms, offering a prompt remedy to our longing for affection. These approaches are not entirely modern. They may appear novel due to the recent development of specific terminology to identify them, which may not have been used in the past. Moreover, with the proliferation of applications and increased connectivity, we actively seek out these forms of expedient companionship. It is akin to obtaining love with a mere swipe on our smartphones—readily available, easily accessible, straightforward, and suitable.

A view cast upon the gay community, there's this idea that we're incredibly free-spirited when it comes to intimacy, finding any place and any opportunity for connection. The notion is that our social lives are vibrant and intense — as if we're constantly chasing the thrill of the moment, living life to the fullest without a thought for the next day. It appears to suit the mindset of a younger individual as well. But in the gay community, we have this added twist: We tend to have this reputation for pursuing excellence relentlessly, no matter what we're up to, always pushing ourselves to meet exceptionally high expectations, arguably more so than our straight friends might. And when it comes to relationships, the conversation can be completely different than our straight counterparts. But there's one commonality between the straight and the gay world, there's no such thing as child abuse when there are two consenting adults. Let me unpack that a bit.

Sex. When two men are involved, there is no fear of pregnancy. Sex can be either intimate or it can be decidedly dirty. You have the choice to decide what type of sexual experience you want, but it's important to understand the rules of the road before venturing down that path. This book will address the prevailing stigmas and strategies for dealing with STDs, describe the appearance of a predator and the potential damage they can inflict upon us, and discuss how apps are shaping our interactions with and perceptions of the world.

Perfectionists. Gay men feel compelled to excel in every endeavor. They must possess all knowledge, witness everything. Even if we've lived half the lives of other people, we're supposed to get cultural references long before our time. We're supposed to have the fanciest things and know all the right people. Success is mandatory, eliciting pride in those around them. As someone repeatedly trapped by these pressures, I recognize the importance of not allowing them to dictate our identity. It is emotion, not material wealth, knowledge, or who you know, that forges our most profound human connection.

Child abuse is undeniably a harsh term in this context, yet it is an undeniable reality in our world. Older individuals exploit their sexual preferences for domination and caregiving to overpower our mental and physical well-being. We entrust our hearts and bodies to these older individuals, believing they are capable of protecting us. However, the sad truth is that they often let us down, leaving us alone to pick up the broken pieces.

If we are unable to identify the potential hazards, what measures can we take to safeguard ourselves? Our future, our emotional welfare, our sense of self-worth, and our capacity to forge robust connections with ourselves and with others are all at risk.

Why is it that these quirky little love habits make us feel like we're back in our teenage years, regardless of our real age? They somehow stamp a youthful vibe on us, but then you've got society lurking in the background, ready to slap the 'immature' label on anyone who's bouncing back from a breakup with a bit of fun, getting their fair share of bedroom action, or just finding love in ways that aren't straight out of a storybook. So, what's the game plan for not coming off as that kid who never grew up? Should we steer clear of it all, keep our love lives secret, or maybe try to flip the script on what everyone else thinks are 'normal'?

Figuring this out isn't a walk in the park. Let's dive in together and explore what society's got in mind for us, the kind of stuff we're at risk for, how choosing the road less traveled when it comes to love might actually be our North Star, and what it's going to take to stand tall, be our true selves, and shed that 'just a kid' skin once and for all.

SOLUTION INTRODUCTION

WE MAY BE YOUNG, BUT WE ARE NOT DUMB.

Sure, do we have to experience things in order to learn from them? Of course. But that doesn't mean blindly going into things without setting the proper expectations or knowing what you're getting yourself into.

This book examines the many situations we commonly encounter. It aids in recognizing predators and the impact they have on our lives. The discussion extends to how sexual relationships skew our perceptions. We explore app intricacies and strategies for effective navigation. The concept of 'situationships' is dissected, pondering their initiation and existence. It warns against toxic signs that prematurely age you. The book encourages breaking free from parental dependence and preventing its spill-over into personal relationships. It identifies the traps that keep you misplaced and hinder your aspirations. We guide you to bolster confidence and embrace our full authentic self. Decisions on whether to avoid or pursuit a situation. Lastly, the book outlines strategies for manifesting your desires and achieving them.

Each chapter is interwoven with the others. At the start of every chapter, there is a quotation that I would like you to bear in mind while reading the section. This book isn't about my life. Should you find parts that do not seem to apply to your experiences, I urge you to persist in reading, as there are numerous shared experiences that may surprisingly resonate with you. This book caters to those who are navigating the complexities of love, whether you are seeking it, are in the throes of it, or simply dissatisfied with your current circumstances. It is intended for you. For the more mature audience, proceed with caution. Some content may feel confrontational, but I implore you to view it as an opportunity for constructive growth.

PART ONE

SITUATION STIGMA

YOU ARE NOTHING TO BE ASHAMED OF.

The need for love is intrinsic in us from the moment of our birth. Without it, a person can develop feelings of bitterness and anger, suffer from depression, and be burdened with a sense of worthlessness. Similarly, a lack of love can sap our motivation to manage tasks, set objectives, and care for ourselves. Love holds the same importance as the daily nourishment we derive from food and the air we breathe. It is crucial that we are at ease with the concept of love, for an absence of comfort in this area hinders the formation of deep, meaningful connections with others, and undermines our sense of self-worth.

Think of how a wedding ceremony looks. The soon to be married couple are at the alter in front of a group of people. The group is facing the married couple. Part of that ritual of the ceremony is the group of people swearing that they will do everything in their power to keep this unity in front of them alive. Whether that happens or not, it is meant to show the support by others. This support is incredibly important as relationships can fluctuate in feelings and when things are bad, it is important to fall back to that support when the people in the relationship do not feel strong enough in that moment. If there is a lack of support, it can lead to physical impacts of mental stress and fatigue. It could also result in bullying and abuse toward others when they don't feel supported themselves.

The concept of belonging can exist to varying degrees, considering the plethora of divergent perspectives on what is considered 'right.' It is both your responsibility and that of those involved to nurture a sense of belonging in your respective worlds. If you were to publicize your relationship on the evening news, you wouldn't find universal acceptance.

However, if you and your companions find a sense of belonging within your local community, amongst friends, and with family, then the beliefs of the wider population are inconsequential. A deficiency in the feeling of belonging can lead to severe depression, anxiety, and, in some cases, can culminate in suicide.

Trust makes everyone feel secure. It gives a sense of safety and boosts confidence levels. Without trust, it can make someone feel insecure and angry. It makes them overwhelmed and uncertain. Without trust, we can't be vulnerable, and vulnerability is a necessity when it comes to forging deep connections.

In order to experience our true selves and recognize our utmost potential, we require the sensations of love and support, a feeling of belonging, and trust.

If we find ourselves lacking in any of these aspects, we do ourselves a grave disservice. We limit the expanse of our potential and fall into an undeserved sense of unworthiness. Often, we mistakenly believe that our ambitions are not legitimate simply because of our youth or because we can't see our progress instantly. Yet, fulfillment is within our grasp. You are deserving of it. Youth does not bar us from knowing love, garnering support, feeling a sense of belonging, or building trust in ourselves and with others.

The Dream: Straight married, two and a half kids, a dog, house with a white picket fence, and a community that fully accepts the marriage. Your parents are high school sweethearts and never got divorced and never cheated on one another. You have been loved all your life but independent enough to take care of yourself. You are completely happy with absolutely no issues or problems to complain about.

Why does this seem like such an impossible fantasy? Well, our parents weren't always there for us. The "marketplace" of people, and our access to one another, through apps has exploded. Our expectations of others and ourselves grew. It seems near impossible finding the right person. We can't wrap our brains around being monogamous unless it's forced on us by a religious entity or societal expectations. And why are there so many affairs and divorces?

At the root of the dream for most people is the same simple desire for **love, support, a sense of belonging, and trust**.

We do what we can to attain and secure these feelings. We discovered that we could have those core emotions whether we are single, casually hooking up, in a situationship, dating, in a relationship with loose rules, in a committed relationship, or married. In some sense, it's liberating to dismantle the stereotype of a happy relationship and redefine what to strive for. But what if, in chasing love, support, a sense of belonging, and trust, you end up limiting what you want and destroy your own happiness or that of others?

Some things we tell ourselves that are seemingly innocent:

- ☐ It's just sex. There are no complications or emotions.
- ☐ It's not going to hurt me, and I just want to relieve this itch.
- ☐ This situationship is fine and I'm temporarily getting what I need.
- ☐ I'm in a relationship and not completely happy.
- ☐ I'm just going to have a side piece but keep this primary relationship and feel fine.
- ☐ I'm married but the sexual energy is gone so I'm going to have an affair to relieve the sexual tension and be content in my marriage.
- ☐ Sex is super complicated. Can sex ever be *just* sex? Do we need to have intimacy and connection [in that form] in order to relieve that itch?

Whatever situation you are in, if you and all involved aren't getting the full love, support, sense of belonging, and trust, then it may be time to reevaluate the situation you are in. If you are feeling any kind of shame, it may be time to reevaluate the situation you are in. If you don't have what you truly deep-down want, then it may be time to reevaluate the situation you are in.

If none of the aforementioned situations apply to you, and everyone involved in your situation is happy, I am delighted for you. You have mastered the art and complexities of love. I am cheering for you. I trust that you will remain happy, and I hope that happiness continues to be a constant in your life.

For those of you who just threw up and feel jealous of anyone who has mastered the art and intricacies of love, or even if you are questioning if you are truly happy, you are in the right place and should totally keep reading.

Craving Love

Why do we crave and need love as humans? It's a basic and fundamental necessity. According to Maslow's Hierarchy of Needs, our requirements are arranged in order: physiological, safety, love and belonging, esteem, and self-actualization[1] . Love ranks above safety yet below esteem, highlighting its essential role in our personal well-being. Robert Sternberg's triangular theory of love outlines the three components of love: intimacy, passion, and commitment[2]. A relationship encompassing only one of these elements is less likely to endure, with two forming a somewhat stronger bond. However, the theory suggests that all three components are essential for a relationship to be truly loving.

We are naturally social creatures and why shouldn't we have that type of love involving support, a sense of belonging, and trust? Support is so important to feel comforted and warm. It helps us deal with life's uncertainties and gives us power to overcome them. A sense of belonging helps us be nicer to ourselves and other people. Trust in a relationship builds confidence and helps us feel safe.

Now, the streets aren't full of people looking like they are loaded on Xanax all the time. We aren't always kind to one another. We have our

[1] Saul Mcleod, P. (2024, January 24). Maslow's Hierarchy Of Needs. Retrieved from Simply Psychology: https://www.simplypsychology.org/maslow.html
[2] BetterHelp. (2024, April 30). What Are The Three Parts of Sternberg's Triangular Theory Of Love. Retrieved from BetterHelp: https://www.betterhelp.com/advice/love/what-are-the-three-parts-of-sternbergs-triangular-theory-of-love/

own perceptions of what it means to be happy and that doesn't always match someone else's.

Feeling Shame(d)

Social stereotypes are annoying. Why can't the world see things as we see it? Or perhaps, why do we feel a self of shame in ourselves? Shame brings feeling of guilt, impact your body image and lowers your self-esteem. People are shamed for being single, casually hooking up, being in a situationship, dating, in a relationship with loose rules, in a commitment, or married. Why? Let's break down each situation and point out what possible shame brings to each.

Let's examine the situation of being single. One stereotype suggests that if you are single, you are not grounded and that something is wrong with you. If you want to change your single status, you may sometimes feel shame. Efforts to find a relationship, such as establishing rules instead of going with the flow, going on multiple dates, or the ways you put yourself out there, are sometimes shamed by others. They believe you don't need to do any of these things to be in a relationship. Nonetheless, these are important steps we take to find our person. By making these efforts, we can be perceived as not being happy on our own. What frustrates me is that much of this shame comes from people who are content with their situation and cannot fully empathize with yours. They have good intentions but just don't understand. If you are happiest being single, you should fully embrace it and overcome the societal expectation of a specific form of happiness.

If you feel ashamed about your casual hookups, it might be best to stop hooking up. If you're no longer interested in hooking up, an important step is to seek the company of individuals who also avoid casual sex. This can foster a sense of belonging and prevent the misconception that casual sex is a universal practice. In gay culture, we often think casual sex is extremely common. We see so many people on the apps and hear countless stories about cruising and guys having random sex with strangers. However, that's not representative of all gay people or the entire population. When we are caught in this illusion or surrounded by those who accept casual sex, we may feel pressured to accept it even if it makes us feel ashamed. This can lead us to view hookups as more common or benign than they actually are, mistakenly believing they represent everyone's desires.

Conversely, if you find yourself shaming others for engaging in casual hookups, it might be because you're projecting your own insecurities and using their actions to boost your self-esteem. Personally, I have shamed others for having casual sex, even though I have engaged in it myself. I realized that my judgment was harmful to both them and me. If I shamed someone for casually hooking up and they already felt ashamed, I was only preventing them from healing. Additionally, my judgment hindered my ability to maintain a positive self-perception.

Instead, we can offer gentle reminders to those who may be straying from their true desires by engaging in hookups. Yet, if you discern that someone is genuinely content and their needs are being met through casual relationships, it's important to fully support their choices.

Let's examine the concept of a situationship. A situationship is not a relationship; it is a romantic connection lacking clear commitments like monogamy or regular communication. Without set boundaries, it is often difficult to navigate and understand. People may feel ashamed of being in such a dynamic because society believes they deserve and inherently want a real relationship. They may be seen as merely settling. However, if all parties set proper expectations and are content with the arrangement, they can overcome societal pressures. Often, situationships are toxic and incredibly difficult to recover from, or they stem from insecurities. It's important to ensure all parties involved are aware of the expectations and fully comfortable with the undefined rules. This can be achieved by asking specific questions tailored to this scenario to everyone involved. Is this what you truly want? If you could change something about the situation, what would it be? Will you feel resentful if this falls apart? Will you be okay if it ends? Are you settling for this, or is this what truly works for you? If there is a negative response to any of these questions, it's crucial to reevaluate the situation to ensure all are receiving love, support, a sense of belonging, and trust.

What happens if you find yourself in a relationship with loose rules? This is somewhat different from a "situationship" because it has some defined boundaries and rules, yet it doesn't fit the typical relationship model. For instance, open relationships have relaxed guidelines. These can work as long as everyone involved feels comfortable with the arrangement and understands the set expectations. However, often someone in this dynamic doesn't fully experience love, support, belonging, and trust. The shame lies in the couple objectifying others and looking outside of the relationship for satisfaction rather than looking inward at each other. It's as if they're masking their own self-worth for the sake of being in a relationship, even if it lacks full love.

Maintaining this dynamic consistently can be challenging for all members. In fact, less than 1% of all couples are in an open marriage. In a 2020 study, about 20% of couples have tried consensual non-monogamy, but open marriages have a high 92% failure rate, with 80% of people in open relationships reporting jealousy.[3] The statistics indicate the difficulty, but maybe you've found a way to make it work. A good way to test if everyone is on the same page is to ask questions like: What do you feel when I am intimate with someone else? If I develop feelings for someone else, how will that affect us? Also, ask the person outside the relationship how they feel, whether they are truly comfortable with the established rules, and if they are getting what they need. If everyone fully feels love, support, belonging, and trust, then face those statistics head-on and work on developing a community accepting of this, ensuring it's well-communicated to everyone to ensure authenticity and confidence.

Let's examine the situation if you're in a committed relationship. Shame in this context is usually directed toward individuals whom others believe should not be in a commitment and might be better off single.

---

[3] Wilkie, N. (2020, October 27). What Is An Open Marriage? And Can It Work? We Asked A Therapist. Retrieved from Red Magazine: https://www.redonline.co.uk/wellbeing/sex-relationships/a34490562/what-is-an-open-marriage/#r3z-addoor

This shame is typically aimed at one person in the relationship rather than both, as society generally values commitment. If you are experiencing shame in your relationship, consider why you are committed and whether you and your partner might be happier in a different situation.

Lastly, let's evaluate the situation of married people. Some individuals frown upon the institution of marriage, often due to high divorce rates, bad personal experiences, or the belief that one shouldn't be with just one person forever. There can also be shame in marriages with clear power dynamics, such as those defined by finances or citizenship. Typically, people in marriages don't feel ashamed, but if you do, challenge others to think about how you and your spouse benefit from marriage and why you wouldn't want to change that arrangement.

Usually, these situations have the best chances for love, support, belonging, and trust because of established rules. However, shame can still exist, and it's important to recognize it to ensure there is a true sense of belonging as well as deep love and support from each other. As you can see, individuals within a commitment or marriage generally experience less shame. This phenomenon arises because society highly regards commitments. Although the degree of this sentiment may vary in each unique situation, it is wise to thoroughly assess both your circumstances and those of others involved.

If you are in one of these categories and say you are happy with it, here's a little test. Are you and the other(s) involved feeling fully and consistently loved? Do you both or all feel deserving of the situation? Can everyone trust each other to not hurt one another? Are you comfortable telling your friends and family about the situation? If you answer no to any of these, then you are not fully comfortable and need to evaluate the situation. Remember, we are innately in need of love, support, a sense of belonging, and trust. If you are not getting these in whatever situation you are in, either choose to strengthen it or change the situation entirely to get what you want.

If you are not happy with the category you are in because you and others involved are not feeling fully loved, being supported, have a sense of belonging and trust, then change either your situation or your own community. We get to choose who we surround ourselves with and it's powerful having an established community accepting of your exact situation.

As mentioned at the beginning of this chapter, if we find ourselves lacking in any of these areas, we do ourselves a great injustice and should change our situation. We limit our potential and fall into the belief that we are unworthy. Sometimes, we incorrectly assume that we are not entitled to everything we desire simply because of our youth or because we do not get it right away. However, such fulfillment is within reach, either by realigning our situation or completely changing it. You are worthy of what you truly want and deserve. Youth does not prevent us from experiencing love, receiving support, feeling that we belong, or fostering trust within ourselves and with others.

APPS

YOU ARE MORE THAN THE PHOTOS AND
VIDEOS POSTED ON A SITE.

Ever since the launch of Match.com in 1995[4], dating apps have exploded. They are a great tool to give you access to many more people at any given time outside of running into someone at the bar or in public. They're incredibly convenient and efficient. You can meet people simply sitting in your living room sofa or in bed. You can filter out people more easily to match your preferences. You can reach specific niche communities and there's a lot less stigma with online dating these days.

While all that sounds great and seemingly innocent, there is a lot to consider when it comes to diving into the apps.

Privacy/Keeping Yourself to and for Yourself

Let's start with the easy one, the leaking of photos and videos. You're messaging with someone, and it gets steamy, and you exchange explicit photos and videos. It's all in good fun. While some apps limit the sharing of that content to a single view and no screenshots, there are usually work arounds or we don't take advantage of the single use share.

You have probably heard of the old saying, "don't text anything you don't want [seen/shown] on the front page of the newspaper." I used to roll my eyes at that and respond like the snarky wise guy I am, "no one reads the newspaper." But then after some personal experience and what

---

[4] Match.com. (2024). About Match.com. Retrieved from Match.com: https://www.match.com/help/aboutus.aspx

my friends endured; I started to listen. What if my family saw it? What if someone at work caught it? Or even worse, someone you genuinely are interested in long term and take seriously sees it? Unless of course the person you shared it with is that person. But what if it isn't?

People are emotional creatures when it comes to love. Jealousy and insecurities creep in. When someone you are trying to build a life with sees you were sharing this kind of content with someone else, it can either be accepted or negatively judged. It's usually accepted in this day and age because we all have done it or some version of it. Read the fine print if it is accepted though. Are they really accepting of it so they can use it as power to go and do it themselves? Would you be accepting of it if they did that with other people? If rejected, learn from what you are putting out there to protect yourself.

Once, I met this guy at a social event, and we really hit it off. We exchanged numbers and kept in touch. About a month later, I got a notification on my phone saying he matched with me on a dating app. I was a bit confused and decided to ask him about it. He told me, "I thought it was kind of cute matching with you on the app." I asked, "Aren't you concerned that I'm on the app?" He replied, "Not at all. I'm on it too. We're all just looking for the best person in our lives, and this streamlines the process."

I started feeling a bit jealous. Usually, I'm very secure, but I began to question if he actually liked me. I wondered if he was just keeping me around until he found someone else. It felt like he hadn't decided if I was right for him, so he stayed on the apps to explore other options. Although I was on the app too, I wasn't active on it. It had been months since I last used it, but my profile still appeared for him. However, neither of us made a decision about each other. Seeing that we were both on the apps made things clear. We eventually drifted apart, which wasn't surprising. We were probably talking to many people and didn't prioritize each other, getting lost in the shuffle of all those different profiles.

In this situation, he accepted that I was on the app, but I couldn't accept him being on it. It actually led me to be more active on the app than to focus on him. Just knowing we were on the apps completely changed the direction of our interaction, so much so that we ended up disconnecting.

Dating apps create a sense of competition. It can be as passive as checking it once a month or being on it every hour of the day. Regardless of how active or inactive you are, someone noticing your presence on the app can trigger all sorts of jealousy. It doesn't matter how often you use it; someone might jump to the worst-case scenario, and it can ruin your interaction. They might feel like they need to compete with others, a feeling rooted in their own insecurities, but it's a very real emotion in the modern dating app landscape.

Even if you aren't active on the apps, your profile can still show up after months of not using them. I didn't realize that you have to log out and/or delete the account, as well as the app, to prevent your profile from being shown. This is intentionally designed to draw you back into the app. They pique your interest with notifications and clamor for your attention to their benefit. What if someone sees your profile, shares it with others, and people start making judgments about you without you doing anything? For many, this isn't an issue, especially if you're comfortable with people knowing you're on the apps, but what if you're not? What if people you don't want to know find out you're on the apps? Think about how you'd feel if those people discovered it without you telling them yourself.

Texting on these apps is so easy. It takes very little effort and can be done at any time. The apps make it incredibly simple with notifications and alerts that draw you in throughout the day, keeping you engaged. You can easily chat with multiple people, which makes it seem like everyone is chatting with more than one person. But can you genuinely create a deep connection knowing you're just one in a lineup? It leaves me wondering, not just about relationships but about what this does to us inside.

Maybe you don't consider yourself to be jealous or insecure. Perhaps you have strong self-confidence and feel proud to show the world you're on the apps. Nevertheless, be aware that these apps come with inherent risks. They expand the user base, which increases the likelihood of users engaging in conversations significantly and results in less privacy for you.

Know that you are essentially broadcasting yourself and your photos as if you're on the front page of a newspaper.

Age

I've noticed that no matter which app you're using, they all seem to share something in common: they want to know how old you are. It's as if giving them your birthday is a non-negotiable requirement. Now, whether that number actually appears on your profile is another issue. But I can't help but feel a bit vulnerable when I think about sharing my age out there.

One issue with sharing your age is that you're opening a door for unsavory characters to potentially find you. It's almost like you're giving a piece of yourself away. Then there's this odd feeling when you realize you might just be mingling in a crowd that's nowhere near your own age. For lack of better options, you end up surrounded by people much older than you. It's like they're the only ones in sight, and you wonder how that even happened.

When I went off to college, it felt like I had picked the quietest corner of suburbia for my studies. Meeting new people was a challenge, especially on dating apps, as the campus wasn't exactly teeming with profiles. So, what happened? I ended up connecting with folks from nearby towns - people much older than my college peers, some even in their own relationships, just looking for a little extra thrill. Almost all of them were much older than me, and I started to feel like only older men found me attractive. I spent a lot of time and energy in this space of older men because that's what the apps were presenting to me.

It's strange, you know? These were the ones noticing me, and I couldn't help but be drawn to them. I wanted to feel validated and loved. I chose searching for this though the apps rather than connecting with my peers on campus for that validation and love. Their attention lighting up my phone and filling some kind of void.

I started to pay less attention to my classmates and more to these distant matches. Reflecting on it now, it's clear how much this skewed the way I saw things. I kind of missed out on the whole college social scene, forming bonds with those I should've been laughing and learning with. I was chasing these moments of validation and sucked myself into a different world. I let an app dictate my focus, and it's something that, in a way, stole a piece of that quintessential college experience from me.

The more we pour our hours into those little squares on our phone, the tighter our world seems to shrink. We find ourselves chasing the fleeting high of each new notification, each digital 'hello' pulling us in like a gravitational force. And somehow, amid the endless scrolling, we miss the chance to look up and notice the actual faces around us, longing for a real connection, yearning for a shared moment in time.

Addiction

Now, let's talk about the ins and outs of dating apps on a personal level. It's so easy to get hooked on these platforms, believing that if you just keep swiping, you'll eventually find someone irresistibly attractive. It's like entering a never-ending beauty pageant. These apps are cleverly designed to keep you paying that monthly fee, all while dangling the promise of love and connection. You'll notice that when you first start using an app, the matches you see are often strikingly good-looking. It's as if they're rolling out the red carpet, showing off their 'top picks' to keep you interested.

When you dive into the world of dating apps, you might find yourself putting your best foot forward—choosing photos in the perfect lighting, crafting a bio that shows off your most appealing traits, and describing what you're looking for in ways that catch the eye. You might gloss over the less flattering parts of yourself, hoping to captivate those stunning profiles you're matching with. Let's be honest, we all do it.

But here's the catch—this can warp your perception of the dating pool. People might post old or overly flattering photos, leading to a gap between expectation and reality. It can become a cycle of letdowns, where the polished profiles you fantasize about don't always translate into real-life chemistry.

You might find yourself constantly swiping, thinking the next person will be "the one," but never truly settling on a match. There's always that nagging thought that there might be someone just a little bit better waiting around the corner.

Predators/People Who Aren't Who They Say They Are

Apps are teeming with fake profiles, leaving you vulnerable to individuals who may not have your best interests at heart or who misrepresent themselves entirely. The lack of stringent vetting processes means virtually anyone can join these platforms. Consequently, the surge in app usage has correlated with a disturbing rise in incidents of sexual assault, robbery, and even murder.

Reports of sexual crimes stemming from first meetings after matching on dating apps soared by 25% from 2017 to 2021. [5]Shockingly, up to 10% of known sex offenders use these platforms to target victims.[6] Even apps that implement background checks reveal alarming statistics: 47% of offenders identified through online dating have prior criminal convictions.[7] Furthermore, there are over half a million online predators prowling these apps every day.[8]

Predators exploit these platforms for their own gratification, using

---

[5] Valentine, J. L., Miles, L. W., Mella Hamblin, K., & Worthen Gibbons, A. (2023). Dating App Facilitated Sexual Assault: A Retrospective Review of Sexual Assault Medical Forensic Examination Charts. Journal of Interpersonal Violence, 38(9-10), 6298-6322. https://doi.org/10.1177/08862605221130390

[6] Matthews, H. (2023, December 14). DatingNews. Retrieved from 27 Online Dating Statistics in 2024: https://www.datingnews.com/industry-trends/online-dating-statistics-what-they-mean-for-future/

[7] National Crimes Agency. (2022, February). Sexual Offences Initiated Via Online Dating Submitted To Serious Crime Analysis Section. Retrieved from National Crime Agency: https://www.nationalcrimeagency.gov.uk/who-we-are/publications/583-online-dating-scas-statistics-2021/file

[8] Child Crime Prevention & Safety Center (FBI Findings). (2024). Children and Grooming / Online Predators. Retrieved from Child Safety: https://childsafety.losangelescriminallawyer.pro/children-and-grooming-online-predators.html

clever manipulation to ensnare their targets. Apps provide an ideal hunting ground for these individuals; with each rejection, they can swiftly move on to the next potential victim, engaging multiple targets simultaneously to streamline their predatory process. While it may not always be evident that you are being preyed upon, rest assured, these predators are adept at hiding their true intentions.

Imagine discovering someone has been deceiving you about their identity only when you finally meet. Or consider the possibility that they've been stringing you along, draining your time and energy for their gain, all the while pretending to be someone they're not. This is the harrowing reality faced by many in the world of online dating.

Apps Are an Energy Vampire

Your time and energy are so valuable. Even if it's through simple texts on an app. The time in-between messages you are thinking of this person, and they could be thinking of you. The rabbit-holes we go down in our minds thinking of someone. The calculus involved when crafting the perfect response. The checking of the app to see if they responded.

We dedicate a significant amount of energy to each interaction that holds potential rewards for us. This energy must be directed intentionally towards individuals who merit our investment. However, with the proliferation of these apps, we disperse our energy across numerous connections, thereby diminishing the value of true connection we might establish with a single person.

We often succumb to the practice of categorizing people and assigning stereotypes to everyone when we use these apps. We tend to overgeneralize. For instance, if we're on a dating app that's known for casual encounters, we might start to assume that this is the universal goal for everyone, forgetting that there are those who are sincerely seeking a committed, long-term relationship. We begin to mistake these platforms for reality. The apps end up setting the terms of what gives people pleasure and fulfillment. This is a big issue as we aren't deciding for ourselves what we want. Instead, these apps present a narrow view of happiness, shaping popular trends and constraining our individual desires.

Women typically "swipe right" merely 30% of the time.[9] Overwhelmed by an influx of messages, they raise their standards, dismissing minor flaws or infractions as they sift through potential matches. Men, contrastingly, often employ a catch-as-catch-can tactic, initially liking numerous profiles before delving into the details more carefully.

For gay men, the quest for commitment can be even more elusive. With Grindr, a commonly used hookup app amongst gay men, boasting over 300 million active users daily.[10] The sight of a screen filled with partially clothed bodies excites users, creating a cycle of addictive orgasms akin to the pull of a slot machine for a gambling addict. Each pull can lead to an immediate hit or a continued succession of attempts, all resulting in a dopamine surge. Imagine that slot machine delivering an orgasm instead of monetary fortune, and you'll see how it can become just as entrancing.

As more gay men succumb to the lure of these apps, the pool of potential life partners significantly dwindles. These platforms shape what people perceive as pleasure and fulfillment, stripping away the opportunity to develop lasting relationships and commitment. When sex enters the equation too early, there isn't sufficient time to cultivate trust, fluid communication, and genuine companionship—vital elements of a healthy relationship.

Seeking a meaningful relationship through these hookup apps is a challenging endeavor. You may find yourself spending time and energy on someone so addicted to these fleeting encounters that the very notion

[9] Florio, G. (2023, February 13). Women Are Much More Selective And Find 80% Of Men Unattractive On Dating Apps, Per Recent Research. Retrieved from Evie Magazine: https://www.eviemagazine.com/post/women-more-selective-80-men-unattractive-on-dating-apps-recent-research#
[10] Arison, G. (2023). Grindr, Inc. Q4 2022 Earnings Call. New York: FactSet callstreet

of commitment becomes alien to them. Their perspective on happiness and value is skewed by the relentless dopamine hits from their digital slot machine. While it may appear that all gay men are solely interested in casual hookups due to the prolific usage of these apps, it's crucial not to have tunnel vision.

One method to distinguish the virtual world of the apps from actual reality is to remind ourselves that the number of people you see walking on the streets in a given area far exceeds the number of profiles you encounter on an app. The app merely reveals who is using it; it does not represent the general population. We must reinforce the understanding that the app encompasses only those who are currently active on it and does not provide an expansive view of the entire community.

A simple exercise involves looking up the population of your current town online. Then, adjust the app settings to only show results within a mileage that encompasses your town's area. Expand your search to include anyone within this specified mileage radius. When you compare your town's population with the number of people using this app within the same area, you'll get a rough estimate of the app's user base relative to the local population. Dividing the two figures will give you an idea of the proportion of residents on the app compared to the overall populace. Of course, there are numerous variables and limitations due to the app's filtering system. However, this will give you a basic insight that the app's user count is significantly lower than the general population. This tells you the app is far from the reality out there.

I know this all sounds terrifying but it's not all bad. I mean it is a great solution in this day of age to meet people. It's amazing for filtering out what you don't want, accessing a broader net of people, and it's incredibly convenient. If you are deciding whether you should hop on the apps or stay on them, just ask yourself a few questions:

How will it make you feel?

Do you feel you are getting what you want out of it?

Do you feel it's a waste of time and energy but somehow so addicted to it?

Are you using the apps as a coping mechanism than to deal with your own issues?

Evaluate what you are looking for and want and adjust accordingly.

When opting to use dating apps, keep these few guidelines in mind for your safety. First, refrain from sharing explicit photos or videos before establishing trust with the other individual. To build that trust, arrange for a video call that allows for a face-to-face conversation. This will enable you to better understand their personality and communication style, as nonverbal cues and spoken language are less susceptible to deceit compared to mere texts.

Also, when planning to meet in person for the first time, it's imperative not to disclose your home address or visit their residence. Instead, choose a public location for the initial encounter. Also, have a contingency plan ready in case the meeting does not progress as anticipated.

We often overlook basic safety rules while using dating apps, which can put our welfare at risk. Giving out your address, for example, exposes you to potential dangers, as you are essentially allowing a stranger access to your personal space—rendering you extremely vulnerable. Consider the imprudence of writing your phone number and address on a restroom stall in a public space; it is equally unwise to share such sensitive information freely and publicly on a dating app.

Furthermore, don't be lured by the appeal of a beauty contest. While we all aim to find the perfect partner, this doesn't necessarily mean the most attractive person. That individual might just be a facade. Additionally, you can't judge someone's character by merely looking at a glammed-up photo. Instead, seek people you would feel comfortable meeting in public. Look for someone who seems relatable and approachable, someone you could see yourself having a conversation with. If this is someone you would likely greet while passing by on the street, chances are you'll be able to have a comfortable dialogue with them through the app.

Dating Beyond the Apps

If you do not want to be on the apps but you want to show you are available, try some other strategies. If you are looking for a relationship, Perhaps consider a matchmaking service where you don't scroll through countless profiles and there's a vetted screening process. If looking for friends and casual acquaintances, perhaps something more passive like taking on a hobby where you can meet other people that have similar interests. I took on Pickleball and have made friends in that entire community just showing up on the court or joining a league. Maybe even an online blog or community that all talk about a specific topic you're interested in.

Whatever path you pick, just remember the importance of the company you keep. It's so true that at this tender stage of our lives, we're incredibly impressionable, almost like clay being molded by the hands that touch us. When we spend time with folks who don't really get us, or who aren't walking a path we want to be on, we start changing without even noticing it. It's like their views and vibes just sort of seep into us. Our lens on life gets a little distorted, and before we know it, we're chasing after an illusion that feels real, but isn't. It's wild how that happens.

SHORT HOOKUPS WITH FAR-REACHING EFFECTS

YOUR BODY IS NOT A LAB EXPERIMENT.

I am certain that at this juncture in your life, you have either participated in a sexual education class or someone has spoken to you about sexual health. However, has anyone ever prepared us for the emotional aspects of sex, and how seemingly innocent behaviors can compromise our long-term prospects and our capacity to form deeper connections?

Back in high school, the idea of sex was intimidating, and I felt completely unprepared. Our sexual education classes mainly covered contraception and the basics of how pregnancy works. It seemed like we were left to figure out everything else on our own. While schools can guide us in many areas of life, I realized that sometimes we need to take responsibility for our own learning. There was hardly any talk about sexually transmitted diseases, the deep emotional effects of sexual activity, or even being gay in my school. It was obvious that many girls were hesitant about having sex for the first time, while boys seemed to treat it like a goal to achieve as soon as they hit puberty. Over time, I've learned that sexual experiences are much more enjoyable and complex than I ever imagined back then.

Sex is far more than a mere physical act. While we might like to think of it as a simple physical need that demands satisfaction—akin to the natural ease of breathing or the necessity of healthy kidney function—it holds a significance well beyond these basic physiological processes.

The stimulation of the genitals activates the brain's dopamine system, which is pivotal for experiencing intimacy. This process allows individuals to discern a partner's scent, taste, auditory cues, and tactile sensations. Additionally, it provides insights into their sense of humor, communication skills, levels of relaxation or inhibition, and whether they exhibit rudeness or aggression. The human brain collects a substantial amount of information when interpreting social cues. Sexual activity results in the release of oxytocin, vasopressin, and dopamine; chemicals that are associated with feelings of love, happiness, trust, and pleasure.[11] This biochemical response can lead to the development of romantic feelings toward a person, even if initial impressions were unfavorable. Biologically, the concept of casual sex is challenged by the inevitable chemical reactions that occur, which foster a connection between the participants. Nonetheless, individuals possess the ability to regulate their emotions and can consciously resist the natural inclination to develop romantic feelings following sexual interactions if they choose to do so.

Some of us may believe physical intimacy with another person is essential. However, it isn't merely the act of engaging in sexual relations that's important. If it were, then the choice of sexual partner would be inconsequential. But clearly, we have specific attractions. What prompts this?

When we feel lonely, disconnected, or in need of support, we yearn for intimacy and emotional closeness. There are countless reasons we might feel this way, but navigating life can be especially challenging if you're going through it alone or don't feel experienced enough. It's important to remember that we all need love, support, a sense of belonging, and trust to forge a strong emotional bond with someone. Sometimes, we try to convince ourselves that a purely physical connection can fulfill these needs. We might think we're finding love in being desired sexually, support through mutual pleasure, belonging through society's acceptance of casual hookups, and trust by sharing

[11] Love TM. Oxytocin, motivation and the role of dopamine. Pharmacol Biochem Behav. 2014 Apr;119:49-60. doi: 10.1016/j.pbb.2013.06.011. Epub 2013 Jul 9. PMID: 23850525; PMCID: PMC3877159.

our vulnerable, naked selves with another person. But does that truly satisfy us, and can it last?

You may be thinking, "I've had purely physical sex without any emotional attachment and enjoyed it a lot." I challenge you to think about it. Ask yourself:

- Did you look for something attractive about this person in order to enjoy it?
- Did you crave it because you were feeling lonely or unsupported?
- Could you have sex with someone ugly or any age?
- Do you feel incredibly guilty or low about yourself after a strictly physical sexual connection?

As you may see, sex isn't just physical. It's incredibly emotional. It's not just emotional for only you either. It's not even just emotional between the parties involved in the physical act itself. It impacts you, the other person(s), and the future people you meet. It may also in some cases impact friends, family, other people associated with you two like if you're both part of a social group like work or the same neighborhood.

Let's explore how casual hookups can influence your capability to meet, date, or maintain a long-term relationship with someone.

Meeting Someone

Imagine the following scenario:

Say you are feeling incredibly lonely one day and you're craving intimacy. You believe the only thing that can make you feel better is to hookup with someone. You look for a random stranger to have sex and invite them over and ends up being a highly pleasurable encounter. However, guilt washes over you as the other person is collecting their belongings to leave. You yearn for them to stay, to cultivate a connection beyond the intense passion experienced in the bedroom, or elsewhere. Yet, they depart leaving you with disappointment and guilt. No contact information was exchanged and uncertainty looms as to whether you have any idea if you'll see this person again.

Time goes on and for some reason you continually revisit the memory of this person with whom you shared a moment of vulnerability with. The session was so intense and passionate, but you find yourself unable to dismiss thoughts of them. Your mind is preoccupied and your focus on other tasks wavers. You struggle to concentrate, whether at work, in the company of friends, or while performing routine tasks that usually require little effort. Throughout the day, your presence is compromised by the lingering thoughts of this person.

This person is still stuck in your mind and all of a sudden someone you haven't met before that is exceptionally attractive to you approaches you. They initiate a conversation, but you somehow find yourself unable to articulate your thoughts or be fully engaged. You're rendered speechless and find yourself paralyzed because this hookup is still in the back of your mind.

Hot stranger: "Hi there. I haven't seen you before, but you look oddly familiar. Do we know each other?"

You: "I don't think so. Maybe"

Hot stranger: "Oh. Sorry to bother asking. I wasn't sure and thought I'd ask"

You: "No worries. Have a good day"

Hot stranger: "You too. Hope to run into you again sometime"

You both leave the encounter and then you wonder why you didn't strike up a conversation with this person. You found them to be incredibly attractive and you're single. But somehow this hot steamy sexual encounter the night before has influenced your potential connection with this person and didn't allow you to explore it in the moment.

Dateability

Imagine a scenario where you meet someone special, let's call him Jack. You two hit it off right away, sparking an engaging conversation that leads to exchanging phone numbers. Soon, you're texting and calling each other, playful flirtations sprinkled in. Eventually, you decide to go on a date, and it turns out amazing. As you spend more time together, your past hookups start to fade away, becoming mere memories as you find yourself really enjoying Jack's company.

Time passes, and things are going so well that you both decide to take your relationship to the next level, experiencing mind-blowing intimacy. You spend the night together and even share breakfast the next morning. You continue to stay in touch, and everything seems to be falling perfectly into place.

Your regular checkup with your doctor approaches. As usual, the doctor orders lab work, and everything appears healthy and normal. You continue with your life, enjoying your daily routine and spending time with Jack. A week later, you receive a call from your doctor's office. Confused about why they are calling; you answer and learn that you tested positive for chlamydia. You need to visit the pharmacy to pick up a prescription. You cannot have sex for two weeks and must follow a daily medical regimen during that time, with a $20 copay for the medication.

Seems like no big deal. You could survive without having sex for 2 weeks and $20 is no big burden. You're also not that worried about taking an antibiotic as long as you can get this disease out of your body. Thank goodness for modern medicine. It really doesn't impact you much but it's just a minor inconvenience.

Now you can't figure out if you got chlamydia from Jack or someone you hooked up with prior. You feel the need to tell Jack to protect him and his health, so you give him a call.

You: "Hey, I just got a call from the doctor's office from my visit last week"

Jack: "Oh? Everything ok?"

You: "Yeah, totally fine. But I did test positive for chlamydia. You may want to get tested and/or treated as well"

Jack: "Oh, no big deal. I'll give my doctor a call and get a test scheduled. Thanks for telling me"

You: "Of course. Are we still on for dinner tonight?"

Jack: "Let's reschedule for tonight. I've got a bunch of things I have to get done. Maybe sometime next week"

Now, you might be wondering if the cancellation was because of your chlamydia diagnosis. Is Jack looking to engage with you only sexually, and upon realizing that isn't an option, decided to cancel? Did Jack view you merely as an object of physical desire? Or could there be someone else in the picture? You long to see Jack, and his absence leaves you with a sense of disappointment, and also now questioning how you will spend your evening.

When we lack all the answers, we sometimes spiral into a whirlwind of thoughts. The only plausible explanation in this scenario is that Jack is disturbed by the chlamydia diagnosis, which could have resulted from a previous hookup. It's much harder to tell someone with whom you've formed an emotional bond than a random hookup.

Before we delve into why you might be feeling this way, let's consider Jack's outlook.

Why does Jack's perspective matter, you might wonder? After all, it is your body, your sexual health, and you're the one investing in treatment. However, Jack is genuinely enjoying your company and feels a strong connection as well. It may have been a long time since Jack had an emotional bond like this with someone. He might find it rare to encounter someone to whom he feels both physically and emotionally drawn. Jack has been willing to alter his daily routine just to be with you. He has dedicated energy, effort, and time. He has shared intensely pleasurable intimacy with you, to the point that it has become habit-forming.

Suddenly, Jack, who hasn't been intimate with anyone else for a while, faces the possibility of contracting chlamydia from you. He begins to ponder whether you're involved with others concurrently or if this stems from a past liaison. There hasn't been talk of exclusivity; it's far too soon for such discussions. Nevertheless, Jack has to adjust to the situation to avoid appearing overly attached or desperate. If so, he may start to emotionally withdraw, prompting you to do the same, leading to a mutual disconnection.

Observe how different these two perspectives are. You suspect Jack is interested in nothing more than physical intimacy, disregards your personal qualities, and possibly has other sexual partners. Conversely, Jack suspects you of being sexually active with others, view this as an unappealing trait since they themselves have been abstinent and feel compelled to emotionally retreat. This mutual withdrawal destroys the budding relationship, and both of you revert to square one.

Hookup, Meet Long Term Relationship

Let's slightly change the scenario between you and Jack: you've had a casual fling with someone who happens to be friends with Jack. Consider the position this places you in. It's tricky, isn't it? Jack might see you as carefree, immature, not quite ready to settle down—more interested in fun than a serious commitment. It feels unfair to be judged that way. After all, don't we all deserve the chance to show our true selves without being defined by a single action?

But let's face it, deep down, we've all been there, making snap judgments, even when we know better. We think we're safeguarding our tender hearts with this kind of thinking, keeping them out of harm's way until someone earns our trust, our commitment. Love's a risky business, and maybe that's just how we cope.

Then there's the other side of the coin. You might end up setting things off-kilter between your past and potential flames. What if the mere thought of Jack's friend and you together is enough to sour the deal before it even starts? Suddenly, the relationship door that once swung wide open starts to nudge closed, bit by bit. It's a poignant reminder, isn't it? If we want to hold on to the hope of something more meaningful, sometimes we need to be a little more guarded about who we let walk through that door. It can really narrow down our opportunities of finding meaningful relationships.

Let's revisit the scenario of potentially transmitting chlamydia to Jack. Perhaps we should have had a more in-depth discussion on the matter and proactively informed Jack about the previous hookup before things got more involved. Better communication between the two of you might have saved the relationship or not gone down the path it did.

You could attribute the misunderstanding to miscommunication, but it's possible that the real problem stems from the hookup you had before meeting Jack. Had that encounter not occurred, it wouldn't have preoccupied your thoughts immediately afterward, potentially damaging the relationship and affecting the emotional well-being of Jack.

This is but one instance in which an ostensibly innocuous fling can obliterate the prospects for a deeper, more intimate rapport with a person worthy of your investment. Let's intensify the potential repercussions to understand how the situation could deteriorate even further.

Imagine the diagnosis wasn't chlamydia, but it was HIV.

Now this hits different. There's no cure for HIV and now you're worried about your own physical health. You're also figuring out how to tell this new person and every person you've had sex with since you were last tested.

Remember my story of how I contracted HIV shown earlier in this book? Try to imagine yourself in my position during that incident. Consider what actions you would take. Would you confide in your family? If so, you would have to admit that you engaged in intercourse without caution. Contemplate whether you would inform your friends, and if they might perceive you differently, potentially altering their behavior toward you. Consider the implications of revealing this to every sexual partner you've had since your last test. Could they become angered by the risk of a permanent illness you've exposed them to? There's a burden of guilt that comes with the possibility of harboring resentment toward the individual from whom you contracted it. Ponder whether you would disclose this to acquaintances at school, those you're not particularly close to, but to whom you might turn for emotional support. There is, however, the risk of them disseminating the information or subjecting you to criticism. How would you broach the subject with future sexual partners, and at what point would you inform them?

Every time I became involved in an intimate relationship, I made sure to inform every past and potential partner about my situation. I believe in the importance of honesty, even when it comes at a personal cost. The fear of potentially hurting someone is a heavy burden for me. It is incredibly challenging to reveal such personal information, but I would rather sacrifice my own comfort than risk causing harm to another person.

My experience in sharing this information often left people surprised and in disbelief that someone my age could face such circumstances. Some did not consider HIV to be a risk factor when engaging in sexual activities with me simply because of my age. On many occasions, they never even asked. Over time, I have learned that I must always take the initiative to disclose my status to protect both myself and them. If you are or want to be more open about issues like this in your current relationships, I suggest you stay tuned to learn more about the importance of doing so and get tips on how to tackle them in part two.

Sometimes, I find that the choices we make in our dating lives, like casual hookups, have a way of echoing back at us. They carry a certain risk, health-wise, and sometimes, they seem to tug at the threads of the deeper connections we yearn for. When I think about it, if what you're really after is that spontaneous thrill, it's important to be mindful of what you're diving into. On the flip side, if your heart is set on finding something lasting and meaningful, steering clear of fleeting encounters could help you stay focused on that goal. It's about protecting yourself, your emotions, and your aspirations for a love that lasts, isn't it?

KINKS/FETISHES

YOU ARE A PERSON, NOT A SEX DOLL.

A kink or a fetish represents desires that lie beyond the typical boundaries of what society considers normally sexually arousing. The key difference is that a kink refers more to a sexual preference, while a fetish leans towards a sexual need. Although these terms might seem similar, it's important for us young adults to grasp the clear distinction between them.

A study conducted on 2,000 Americans by the sex toy brand EdenFantasys has yielded significant insights into the prevalence and nature of sexual fetishes and kinks. The data indicates that over a third of Americans acknowledge having a particular kink or fetish. Role playing emerges as a prominent interest in the realm of bedroom activities, with 29% expressing interest and 24% considering engaging in it with their current partner. Furthermore, 51% of respondents reported possessing a fetish or distinct sexual interest, noting that it generally takes at least a month or longer for them to divulge this to their partner. Interestingly, 14% disclosed their fetish after just one night with a new partner. Additionally, 37% of participants indicated that they had encountered a partner with a specific kink preference and had subsequently experimented with it themselves.

It's pretty eye-opening to realize that one in three Americans has a sexual fetish or kink. A recent study points out that a fetish, which is essentially a sexual need, is something 51% of people take at least a month to open up about, while only 14% are willing to share after just one night.[12] This really highlights how rarely we talk about these things, and there are plenty of reasons why. Maybe it's because society considers them taboo and there's a real fear of being rejected. Or perhaps we worry about putting the other person in an uncomfortable situation, so we keep it to ourselves. And then, there's the unsettling thought that these fetishes might sometimes be used by more unscrupulous individuals in ways we don't often consider.

There are countless kinks and fetishes and what constitutes a kink or a fetish changes over time, but I want us to focus specifically on age play kinks and racial fetishizing. We should explore how these can affect us emotionally and influence our ability to form deeper relationships.

Age Play: An "Innocent" Fetish?

Age play is a specific type of role-playing scenario in which an individual enacts behaviors or treats another individual as if they belong to a different chronological age category with a clear power dynamic. It's incredibly psychological. This may manifest through the accentuation of certain age-related traits. Typically, one participant assumes the role of a child, while the other adopts the role of an adult, creating a dynamic centered on the differential age representation. I know it's not one of the harshest or crudest fetishes out there, but it is something that impacts us.

I used to think the terms daddy and boy were such a turn on. Then I realized what it really meant and how impactful those words are. The dad is typically the dominate, smarter, caretaker to the young boy who is inexperienced, submissive, and needing help. I have criticized many overusing these terms because it's assigning a stereotype and belittles both parties. I've said to older men, instead of calling you daddy, can

---

[12] Schmmall, T. (2018, February 1). Many Americans Too Shy To Reveal Sexual Fantasies To Partners, Says Study. Retrieved from Fox News: https://www.foxnews.com/food-drink/many-americans-too-shy-to-reveal-sexual-fantasies-to-partners-says-survey

I call you gramps? They laugh but then they realize they are making themselves older calling themselves daddy. No one wants to be someone's grandfather sexually.

Being a boy is degrading. Historically, slave owners called their slave workers boys. When used sexually, this should not be a turn on. It belittles your self-worth and who you are as a person. You are not a slave to someone. Even in its kinkiest form, it's extremely dangerous to allow someone to have that power over your body and mind. Even if you trust someone to have that kind of power over you, it isn't going to be who you are. You shouldn't allow someone to dictate who you are as a person; you should have the power to do that for yourself.

It's important to acknowledge that sometimes, the experiences of your 'youth' may surpass those of an individual who has lived a longer life. You might be 40 years old, but the question remains: have you truly lived those 40 years, or have you merely repeated the same patterns every year without any personal growth? A person of 20 years may possess more life experience than one who is 40. The essence lies not in number of years you lived, but rather in the richness of your experiences that foster growth and in your responses to them. Reflect upon this: what unique experiences have you undergone that are unparalleled or that someone older might never encounter?

Daddy

The 'daddy' is the type of older dominate caretaker that is supposed to be the boss of someone, a caretaker, showing power, and masculine. I'm not talking about a type of pedophilia but just the run of the mill societal acceptance of the term daddy in sex.

In the early 17th century, prostitutes used the term daddy referring to their pimps. The older person setting up sexual customers for their prostitutes were referred to as daddy. In this context, the caretaking daddy was responsible for offering their 'children' for sexual favors in return for money.

Society has normalized using the term "daddy" to describe an older, attractive man in a sexy way. Marilyn Monroe, a superstar of her time, popularized phrases such as "am I your good girl, daddy?" and "every baby needs a daddy." This playful use of "daddy" has found its way into comedy, fashion branding, and hit songs we adore. The cheeky question, "who's your daddy?" prompts more giggles and flirtation than criticism. It's so embedded in our culture now that we rarely consider it a fetish anymore. But how did this term make its way into our bedroom?

The Teacher and the Student

Back in Ancient Greece, Plato, a renowned philosopher, often vividly described his teacher Socrates in his writings. Socrates had a unique way of teaching that sometimes-blurred boundaries. He could become overwhelmed by desire when in the presence of his handsome young students, often implementing careful measures to avoid compromising situations – no embracing, and kisses were lessened to simple pecks.

Plato even described himself as 'boy crazy' in his writings, shedding light on the complicated dynamics of their relationships. Tragically, Socrates was eventually executed on charges of corrupting the youth of Athens. Though there was no specific law at the time, he was accused of leading young men astray both morally and sexually, and allegedly even driving some into prostitution.[13]

A subset of the age play kink is a role play scenario involving an intimate relationship between a teacher or professor and a student role. In this subset, the teacher is essentially grooming the student in a sexual manner. What happens if you have a teacher kink? Is that, ok? The problem lies when you start getting feelings for your actual teacher. It would violate the school's policy with these kinds of relationships.

[13] N. Smith, R. Jones and R. Sharma, eds., The Bloomsbury Companion to Socrates, Second edition, Bloomsbury Press

Sometimes it's against the law. If it was ok to act on this kink, why do these policies exist?

Teachers may not naturally come off as sexy, but there's something about the idea of them that fires up our imaginations. Society tends to paint them as alluring figures, often featuring them in mainstream erotica and adult films. Many men, particularly those between 18 and 24, find themselves drawn to this fantasy. According to RedTube, men in this age range are 80% more likely than others to search for videos featuring seductive teachers.[14] There's a certain appeal in the way we perceive them as attractive caretakers, making that connection all the more enticing.

When a teacher and a student are involved in a questionable relationship, it's often because the teacher holds more power, making the student more susceptible to harm. The law strictly prohibits any form of sexual misconduct by educators, even if the student is legally old enough to consent. Such actions can lead to the teacher being arrested and prosecuted, facing severe consequences including a Class C felony charge. A Class C felony is incredibly serious, on par with crimes like arson, burglary, voluntary manslaughter, and even murder. It ranks as the third highest in severity.[15]

It's not uncommon for kinks to be taboo, yet they can steer our young minds towards infatuations with our teachers. We may unknowingly chase relationships that echo that dynamic of someone caring for and guiding us. When we feel an attraction to people much older than ourselves, it's often because we're seeking something familiar, something we crave but have been missing. Sometimes, we catch ourselves feeling excessively jealous or possessive, as if we're terrified of losing someone's attention. The fear of abandonment hangs over us, trapping us in a repetitive, harmful cycle. These are classic signs of what's often called "daddy issues." Whether

---

[14] Weismman, C. (2020, March 19). Why Are Grown Men Still So Hot For Teacher? Retrieved from Fatherly: https://www.fatherly.com/love-money/why-sexy-teachers-are-still-so-damn-hot

[15] Abboud, M. et al., "Educator Sexual Misconduct: A Statutory Analysis." Criminal Justice Policy Review, 2020. Vol.31 (1) 133-153.

we're drawn to teachers, father figures, or other authoritative individuals, understanding all aspects of this can help us protect ourselves.

Boy

Being the boss, a caretaker, showing power, and exuding masculinity may sound appealing. We've discussed the dynamic of the dad/older figure, so let's explore the opposite end of this fetish—the boy role. The submissive, the one who follows orders and learns from the daddy counterpart. Why isn't this aspect talked about much? Why is being the boy not considered as sexy or hot?

This part of the fetish does not get blown up in the media as much because the idea of people pretending to be little boys is often uncomfortable. There's an attractiveness to the thought of being nurtured and protected, but the notion of regressing to a childlike state to get such tenderness can feel quite unsettling.

Before we get into the childlike state, let's go into why it's important to be nurtured and protected for sex. Without safety, there is no vulnerability. There is absolutely nothing else more vulnerable than giving your body to someone physically.

Stephen Porges, PhD, a trailblazer in neuroscience and a top authority on the autonomic nervous system, presents an intriguing theory. He explores how this system influences our sense of safety, trust, and closeness through a component known as the social engagement system. According to Porges, when we feel secure, our social engagement system allows us to connect, listen, empathize, and collaborate. It also fosters creativity, innovation, and courageous thinking—qualities that strengthen our relationships. Conversely, when our minds sense danger, it triggers a survival response, causing us to become withdrawn, tense, defensive, or irritable, which can strain our relationships. This process of sensing safety or danger, known as neuroception, happens beyond our conscious awareness. Porges illustrates how our nervous system uses bodily sensations to gauge risk and safety. When we sense safety through neuroception, our social engagement system promotes warmth and connection. But when we detect danger, all our focus shifts to assessing and protecting ourselves.[16]

Sex is typically much more vulnerable for women than it is men. Men are seeking for acceptance while women are seeking for trustworthiness. A man will ask, will this woman have sex with me? A woman will ask, can this man be trusted?

She asks this for many reasons but one of the biggest is the fear of getting pregnant. Whereas men do not run this risk, they are less vulnerable. Women, subject to physical penetration in PIV (penis in vagina) sex, bear the potential for pain. He ought to provide support, extending additional tenderness and care during this time—a level of attention he may require less, given his less sensitive nature in that regard. Moreover, women engage in substantially more effort in matters of sexual intercourse.

Straight men often wonder if they're seen as attractive and dependable in a woman's eyes. Can I prove my masculinity and strength to her, in a way that assures her I'm someone she can rely on? When I think about her, her mind, her body – they're precious, and I want her to see that I'm capable and willing to cherish and protect them both. Once a condition of security is evident, vulnerability may ensue, permitting both individuals to engage in intimacy.

In age play, in the gay world, two consenting men, the dad and boy, it isn't as vulnerable as a man and woman. While there isn't a fear of pregnancy but there is a fear of pain and need for tenderness. It is paramount for the male youth to experience a sense of security, given that his susceptibility to vulnerability might greatly surpasses that of his elder paternal counterpart. It is extremely difficult for the person who is supposed to take on this submissive role to not feel like the submissive person when they are told that is the role they are. As previously stated, without safety, there is no vulnerability. Vulnerability is essential to the part that is playing the boy in this fetish.

---

[16] Porges, S. (2024). How To Feel Safe, Secure & At Peace. Retrieved from Good Life Project: https://www.goodlifeproject.com/podcast/how-to-feel-safe-secure-at-peace-stephen-porges-seth-porges-vegus-nerve-ployvagal/

Besides pain, what makes the boy more vulnerable? Calling someone a "boy" can feel diminishing, as if you're implying, they can't stand on their own two feet. It's as though you're saying they're not quite capable of handling life without someone hovering over their shoulder. It strips away their dignity, reducing them to someone who's in constant need of guidance and can't possibly take care of themselves. It's a personal hit that unfairly deflates their sense of self-worth. It is important for the "boy" to not feel personally attacked in order to engage sexually but whose responsibility is that? The boy or the dad?

In a heterosexual relationship, it is the man's duty to make the woman feel safe. So, it's reasonable to assume that in the age play fetish within the gay community, the 'daddy' should ensure the 'boy' feels secure, correct? They are supposed to be the caregiver in this dynamic. However, sometimes the daddy doesn't prioritize the boy's safety. This is often evident in older men seeking younger partners for no-strings-attached flings or in open relationships seeking additional thrills. To prevent our neurotransmitter receptors from triggering survival responses, the boy needs to establish a sense of safety.

How does a boy create a sense of self-security? The harsh reality is, they often don't. Sometimes, we look around and see that this lack of security is normalized by society, and we convince ourselves that we can manage with minimal safety or vulnerability. Because there's no fear of pregnancy and sometimes pain can bring pleasure, the need for security starts to seem unnecessary. We might think we're safe because society deems certain situations acceptable, but our bodies tell a different story. When we don't feel safe, we shut down—we avoid connecting, engaging, or offering the emotional warmth that relationships need to grow.

Seeking Pleasure in Pain

When we start seeking pleasure in pain, we believe we are deserving of this pain and lower our self-esteem. We can become masochistic which are those getting pleasure from experiencing pain and humility. The boy feels they are deserving of this pain and humiliate themselves for the good of the daddy or older figure. We are also putting ourselves at danger. We live temporarily in this fantasy world and forget about real life for a moment.

Young men are frequently burdened with demeaning monikers, including "fuckboy," "good boy," "son," and "twink." Such labels serve to reinforce the authority of the so-called "daddy" rather than empower the "boy." When the younger individual adopts these names, they may begin to internalize them, allowing the titles to shape their identity and perceived value. Subsequently, they risk becoming the embodiment of the stereotypes each label carries. The label "fuckboy" suggests a person who is promiscuous and deemed unworthy of meaningful relationships. The term "good boy" implies worthiness only through servitude to the "daddy." Being called "son" suggests a perpetual state of dependency, incapable of equal status or significance. Lastly, "twink" implies an expectation to be fragile and slender, subject to subjugation and control by the "daddy."

Adopting such titles compromises our ability to be taken seriously, thereby reducing our value and leading us into the trap of accepting this as our fate. It reinforces the notion that we only achieve success and significance through these labels. While the temporary satisfaction may seem appealing, it ultimately harms your reputation and restricts your aspirations in the world. These titles often impede the development of deep, meaningful relationships as they invite ridicule rather than respect when one attempts to engage in serious matters.

Age play can be seen in two ways: as a kink or as a fetish. It's a kink when it's just a sexual preference, but it becomes a fetish when there's a need to be in an older/younger relationship. By making age play a fetish, we close off the chance of finding a peer. We become fixated on being in a relationship with a significant age difference, which limits our chances for connection. When we restrict ourselves like this, we miss out on the full potential of what we could have, focusing only on what we believe suits us. The true reason why we turn it into a fetish lies within us. Are we pursuing these relationships because we've truly figured out what works for us, or is it a deeper self-esteem issue where we think only older people will find us attractive? Have we become so immersed in the kink that it morphs into a fetish because it's the world we've surrounded ourselves with, never considering any other possibilities?

Sometimes, because of the very nature of kinks and fetishes, these experiences can become secretive. You might find yourself in a sexual encounter or relationship that you keep hidden from the public eye, driven by a fear of societal rejection. If the involvement is just a casual hookup rather than an established relationship, the risks grow even more because it's easier to hide a hookup. This secrecy can snowball, making all your relationships, whether casual or serious, hidden from view. When we can't see or talk about what's happening, think about how that could slowly erode your sense of self.

Sometimes we tell ourselves that everything is fine, but deep inside, we know a different story. Initially, these feelings seem harmless, but if we're honest with ourselves, they chip away at our core. Maybe we don't want to be belittled by various titles or nicknames. Maybe deep down, you don't want to be serving someone older. Perhaps you'd rather be with someone your own age but are too afraid to explore that path. Or maybe you keep your relationships hidden to avoid judgment. If these feelings are eroding our self-esteem, they'll soon damage the meaningful connections we crave. It's like those little indulgences we can't resist, even though they can ruin the dreams and goals we hold dear. We often convince ourselves that we deserve this, but maybe what we really need is to step out of our comfort zones and realize that we might be seeking comfort in our pain rather than genuine pleasure.

Racial Fetishizing

Some people claim they have a 'personal preference' when it comes to dating men of certain ethnicities. This race-based fixation on specific physical traits can both idolize and demonize racial differences. A study, which involved 858 unique profile screenshots and 26 in-depth interviews with users of popular gay apps like Grindr, Scruff, and Jack'd, revealed that racial fetishizing is rarely explicit in public profiles, though men of color often experience it more frequently. As a result, these men described feeling objectified, finding it difficult to form platonic or intimate connections, and feeling reduced to mere stereotypes.[17]

Racial preference means being drawn to someone because of their race, culture, religion, environment, or background. It often stems from a shared understanding of the challenges someone might face, leading to a deeper connection. This preference focuses on the individual without relying on stereotypes. On the other hand, a fetish occurs when this preference becomes an obsession with seeking out people of a certain race. This shift can make it more about society's view than the person themselves. When preference or kink turns into a fetish, it often involves an idealization or demonization of racial differences.

It can be deeply discomforting when someone approaches you saying, "Your uniqueness is captivating to me," or "Your rich, brown skin is absolutely striking." Sometimes, they'll say, "You're the first black person who's ever caught my eye," or even, "There's an amazing smell about you, reminiscent of spices and chicken curry." If you have to be described as a color or even food, you're being fetishized. You're an object of fascination rather than a person.

The term "boy" in this particular context has an even more significant pejorative connotation. When an individual of Caucasian descent utilizes this term to address a person of color, it implies a sense of superiority. It reduces status that is not on par with their own. This usage reflects underlying racial biases and perpetuates a legacy of inequality.

It's a deeply personal and complex issue. Imagine being referred to as a "boy" when you're a grown man, and on top of that, your dark skin color becomes another layer to consider. Could this intertwine with someone's age play or racial fantasy? It's a troubling thought that brushes

17 Stacey L, Forbes TD. Feeling Like a Fetish: Racialized Feelings, Fetishization, and the Contours of Sexual Racism on Gay Dating Apps. J Sex Res. 2022 Mar-Apr;59(3):372-384. doi: 10.1080/00224499.2021.1979455. Epub 2021 Sep 22. PMID: 34550047.

dangerously close to echoes of slavery, and that's something incredibly sensitive and loaded with history. In writing this book, I didn't set out to focus on matters of race and ethnicity, yet I can't help but pause at the way the word 'boy' crops up, almost with a certain infatuation, in both realms. It's a peculiar thing, isn't it? How such a term can strip us bare to our cores, leaving us exposed/vulnerable, feeling unsafe and somehow diminished in our own eyes.

When all these various scenarios infiltrate our bodies and overwhelm our minds, we forfeit control over our fate. They are not reality, nor are they meant to be. In actuality, when kinks and fetishes manifest in real-life relationships, they become subject to judgment. Such judgment is unjust, especially when both individuals strive to live an authentic existence with one another. Yet should they engage in these kinks and fetishes without establishing equality or acknowledging the younger individual's strengths, the dynamic can become harmful and toxic.

OLD MEN AND PREDATORS

YOU ARE A HUMAN BEING, NOT A SEX DOLL.

What is a predator?

Have you ever been checked out by someone and just felt gross afterwards? Were you alone in a situation where someone is trying to invade your space when you don't want them to? Have you ever felt that someone is exploiting you mentally? Have you been cat-called or inappropriately complimented by someone? If you are feeling any of these, more than likely, you are being preyed on.

Predators actively seek sexual gratification with individuals who possess less social, financial, or physical power than themselves. Typically, they target those who crave attention and need someone to listen to them, often employing an aggressive approach. While their actions may not always break legal boundaries, their behavior is undeniably inappropriate. Their motives go beyond the mere pursuit of sexual activity; they use sexual interactions as a means of establishing dominance and exerting control. These predators aim to feel powerful and control someone else to achieve an emotional high, rather than controlling their own urges. Such individuals commonly prey on younger persons, as these targets are more vulnerable and generally align with the predator's objectives.

Predators chase because they want something from you. Whether it's your body or to control you, it isn't good. Their signs of love can be misleading because it isn't about who you are as a person that drives this kind of predatory behavior. It is their own want and need to control someone else to satisfy their sexual manner. They will not value your mind or experiences. You have so much to offer. Do you want someone to take your mind and experiences away from you just for their own selfish benefit?

What are some signs that you have been preyed on or being preyed on?

A classic sign that you may be being preyed upon is the creation of dependence, which is a form of manipulation. They overwhelm you with frequent calls, messages, gifts, and compliments. You might start to think that this kind of affection is unmatched, that only they can provide it. This cultivates your loyalty and vulnerabilities, which they exploit for their gain.

Additionally, manipulation manifests in the form of gaslighting. They might present you with distorted information, prompting you to question your own thoughts and the surrounding circumstances. They aim to sow seeds of doubt regarding your memory, perception, and even your sanity. Utilizing these insecurities, they craft their own narrative, persuading you to accept it as truth.

Those with predatory tendencies may exhibit jealousy or attempts to exert control. They may obsessively oversee your activities, restrict your interactions with others, and gradually constrict your world.

Sometimes, we may think predatory behavior only comes from strangers. However, it can also come from someone with whom you are in a relationship. Perhaps the person you're involved with is controlling you and not treating you as an equal. Maybe they know you crave attention and use that knowledge to make you dependent on them. They might even gaslight you, ensuring they win every argument while hiding the truth about certain things.

We might attract this type of behavior if we don't establish boundaries. Without proper boundaries for ourselves and others, these predators will keep pushing them further. By continually granting consent, you enable the continuation of such predatory practices. In doing so, you inadvertently allow this person to exploit you for their sense of dominance and control, which diminishes your self-worth and granting them sway over your life.

Consensual Age Gap Relationships

We often think that whenever there's a big age gap in a relationship, it's just an older person taking advantage of someone younger. But there are times when both people have qualities that put them on equal footing, without one having all the power over the other.

In a recent study, the differences in age within couples were highlighted. It was discovered that 8% of male/female couples have an age gap of 10 years or more. This percentage increases to 25% among male/male couples and 15% for female/female couples. The study also delved into the relationship dynamics between each individual and their father, finding no significant differences between homosexual and heterosexual father-son relationships. For gay men specifically, strained relationships with fathers were often linked to gender identity issues rather than their sexual preference for male partners.

It's commonly thought that gay men who find themselves in relationships with significant age differences might have had problematic relationships with their fathers, but the data doesn't support this assumption. In fact, despite the higher occurrence of age-gap relationships among gay men, their relationships with their fathers were no different from those of their straight counterparts.[18]

So, if these relationships aren't about father issues, what drives this attraction? In this chapter, we'll explore the reasons behind the allure of older partners, why older individuals might seek younger partners, the implications of terms like "daddy" and "boy," and how to steer clear of predatory behavior to maintain control in these relationships.

---

[18] Pew Research Center. (2013). A Survey of LGBT Americans. Pew Research Center.

Age, Not Just a Number

Let's start with a person's age. There are several ways to measure a person's development: biological age, psychological age, superficial age, and social age. Biological age is easy. It's not subjective. You can't change a person's biological age. All these other ages can change. Psychological age would essentially be a person's maturity age. How they have grown as a person physiologically. Superficial age is how old/young does that person physically look. Social age is someone's age compared to their social norm/culture expected of them.

Let's break down one of the subjective ages that changes over time, psychological age. This age can change and vary over time. One way our physiological age can greatly change is through a dramatic life event. Let's use for example a death of a parent. I lost my dad, and I could have reacted in many ways. I was not close with my dad so I could have ignored it was happening which would have lowered my psychological age.

Or, I could have gone through the emotions involved with losing a parent and learn from the experience which would boost your psychological age. This is when we become more mature stretching further than our biological age. Other characteristics of a psychological age is manners and respect for others. An older psychological age can be saying please and thank you, understanding where someone else's emotional state is and sympathize, being friendly to others even if they aren't friendly back. A lower psychological age is disrespecting others, being too involved in their own life to be bothered by anyone else's, being mean and disrespectful to others.

We can boost our physiological age by ways of therapy, hard life lessons, social conversations, and opening our minds to others. Conversation is such a powerful tool by which to alter your psychological age. Who you talk to has such a huge influence on your life and can help you either grow as a person or deter your growth. You get to decide who in your life you can have conversations with and how they'll impact your life. Choose wisely.

Superficial age is far more complex than we often realize. I get Botox injections and work out every day. I'm proud to say I have a great body because I work hard on it. I am careful about what I put into my body and research nutritional methods to help me look my best. Have you ever heard someone at the gym say that someone has a great body because they are young? I hear it constantly, and it drives me crazy because it disregards all the effort I put into my body. We don't have a certain kind of body just because of our age. Our build is influenced by genetics, nutrition, and activity. Is it easier to have a fit body when you are young? We might have more energy due to a more efficient aerobic metabolism, allowing us to be less fatigued from high-intensity exercise and recover faster because we produce less lactic acid compared to older individuals. We may also have a higher metabolism than older people because muscle loss with age slows down the metabolism. But we all know some really fit older people who do not look their age because of how they prioritize their looks and health.

Social age is an indicator of how a person relates to others within the context of their society. For example, a 12-year-old in an ancient society might have been on the cusp of adulthood, whereas today in the West, that cusp is more typically between 20 and 25 years old. Some indicators of social age could be someone's financial status, career, responsibilities, and emotional intelligence.

Think of these age categories like different pieces of a puzzle. Each piece, when examined on its own, offers a glimpse into a specific part of a person's life. But when you put all the pieces together, you get a composite picture that I like to call their dating age average. Let me walk you through it.

Sometimes it feels like different parts of our age are in conflict with each other. Consider being 60 and enjoying graphic tees from a trendy teen store, despite the expectation to dress more professionally. You might overhear people whispering, "Aren't they too old to wear that?" This is an instance where our chronological age and social age don't align. Picture a doctor who should appear clean-cut but proudly displays a neck tattoo. Someone might remark, "Aren't they too mature for that tattoo?" This is an example of physiological age clashing with superficial age. Or, if you're 17, managing to be financially independent, excelling in school, and essentially taking care of yourself – that demonstrates a maturity beyond your years. Yet, you might still react intensely to rejection. This illustrates your social age clashing with your physiological age

Ever thought about how the age of the people someone dates might tell a story? It's fascinating because it can reveal if they're wise beyond their years or still growing into themselves. By looking at this dating age average, we get a glimpse beyond their biological age, perhaps giving us a clue about whether someone might be on the same wavelength as us for a potential relationship.

In this exercise, we look at different aspects of a person's growth in three areas - physical, outward appearance, and social interactions. We assign an age to each area based on their development. By averaging these three subjective ages, we can determine a "dating age" which might not match your actual biological age.

I'll use myself as the first example. Ronek is 32 years old. I get Botox regularly and have a muscular, fit build that makes me look 27. I attend weekly therapy sessions, constantly improving my ability to form stronger relationships compared to those who are 35 years old. I have a great job that provides me with financial independence and expectations to fit into a corporate mold, which most people achieve when they are 40 years old.

Biological age: 32
Superficial age: 27
Physiological age: 35
Social age: 40

Dating Age Average: 27+35+40 = 102/3 = 34

Result: I am slightly older than my biological age.

Let's consider Greg, a 55-year-old man who meticulously maintains his appearance. Greg is dedicated to his fitness routine, undergoes cosmetic procedures, eats a healthy diet, and even sports a tattoo sleeve, all of which make him look 40. However, he is highly emotional and prone to outbursts. He prefers texting over talking on the phone and exhibits significant impatience. His inability to form logical or rational thoughts gives off the impression of a 20-year-old. While he doesn't earn a substantial income, he manages to live comfortably in his studio apartment, covering all his bills and maintaining little debt, much like someone who is 35.

Biological age: 55
Superficial age: 40
Physiological age: 20
Social Age: 35

Dating age average: 40+20+35 = 31

Result: Bill is younger than his biological age.

We can use this exercise when figuring out if someone is the right match for us to date. It goes beyond just looking at their age, delving deeper into our overall compatibility. Let's imagine I'm thinking about dating Greg, who is 55 years old, while I'm 32. The biological age difference is pretty big, but our dating age average align surprisingly well, with mine being 34 and his being 31. This suggests that I could actually consider dating Bill, who isn't a real person I've been involved with. Our dating ages are similar, so we might balance each other out nicely. After all, opposites often attract and fit well.

Try this exercise on yourself and with those you know well. Ask them to try it on you and compare. Do you discover that you thought you were younger than you actually are? Do you realize you are older than your age? Are you surprised at the difference between the two? Once you feel confident that you have the right dating age compared to your biological age, ask yourself if you are comfortable with that. If not, what can you do to change this?

If you want to alter your superficial age, change your exercise regimen and evaluate what you eat. You could also get surgery or try minor appearance related solutions like creams to alter your appearance. You could also dress a certain way. We look younger when wearing athletic outfits but look older in a suit.

If you want to alter your physiological age, consider who you are close to and spend a lot of time talking to. These people influence your life. Do you typically get close to older mature people or younger immature people? A therapist can carefully evaluate and provide tips on how to properly align your physiological age as well. Your social age can be altered by how you relate to certain generations. You can research generational stereotypes and try to learn more about that specific generation and align yourself to it.

Whatever age you are for each of these categories is specific to you and there should be no judgement on how you land for each. It's just who you are, and you should not feel ashamed for being the awesome you that you are. Try to be as truthful to yourself and allow others to be truthful with you in order to properly evaluate how you stand.

Now that we have evaluated the various ways age can be measured, let's talk about older people.

The Chase

I've learned that sometimes we end up dating people older than ourselves. For me, this was partly because my dating age felt out of sync with my actual biological age. After many failed relationships and numerous therapy sessions, I've come to realize the importance of being with someone who is more or less a peer. It fosters mutual respect and helps avoid any controlling dynamics. That's not to say dating older is always the wrong choice—there can be good reasons for it. But before diving into such a relationship, here are a few things to consider and some questions to ask yourself.

Why do older individuals pursue younger ones? The allure of youth captivates them; they seek companions whose biological and subjective ages mirror their own perceived youthfulness. However, this description may be overly sanitized. To view it from different perspectives, they yearn to recapture the essence of youth. They desire to feel desirable and to embody the vibrant energy that people their own age, lack.

Let us delve further into the chase. Imagine an older person wanting to shape the mind of someone younger. They might not have kids and deep down wish they did, or perhaps they feel their parenting skills weren't up to par. There could be an emptiness in this person's life. Maybe they always dreamed of being a caretaker but never had the chance to have a child. Or perhaps they do have a child, but the relationship isn't strong, so they turn to you as a way to fill that gap.

This older person might be at an age where they start to panic about growing old, prompting a desire for a younger companion to stave off those feelings. They may want to stay connected to younger culture and feel youthful again by being with you.

In both of these scenarios, there might be a tendency to be overly controlling. This can affect your self-esteem, as your unique traits might not be the primary reasons for their interest in a relationship with you. You could feel pressured to be a surrogate child or to appear more youthful, fitting into a stereotype rather than fostering a healthy, balanced relationship. This dynamic can trap you in a 'boy' state rather than an equal relationship.

Regardless of the reason, their attraction to you might extend beyond who you are specifically. This isn't to say you aren't attractive—because you certainly are. However, their level of attraction to you might encompass something more than just your individual traits. Ask yourself if this attraction is part of a midlife crisis and might be short-lived, or if it's something they desire for the long term. You can ask an older person their opinion, but they may lie, be defensive, or tell you the truth. In any case, observe their actions, words, and behaviors. This can be very revealing once you delve into their history and current emotional state.

Why do we chase older people? In my own case, I was always chasing older people and making long term relationships work with them.

It wasn't just because of my dating age being higher than my biological age based on the exercise above. It went deeper than that. After years of therapy and a deep dive into my past, my desire to be with an older person was an underlying father complex.

I didn't really delve into my strained relationship with my father in the 'My Story' section of this book. I saved that for the part where we discuss relationships. Here's a brief overview of my father: During my childhood, he had an affair. Wanting to be with multiple women, which my mother couldn't accept, she decided to divorce him when I was in the fourth grade. Even after the divorce, he continued his pattern of infidelity with various partners. His mind was so occupied with these other relationships that he didn't have the time or emotional capacity to give me the affirmation I longed for as a child. Because of this, I never felt comfortable sharing my secrets or my life with him, including my relationships with men. As I grew older, I ended up seeking out older men, trying to find the validation I had missed from my father. I searched for a better father figure and made sure they were loyal to me in a monogamous relationship and demanded more attention than was healthy or fair. While seeking validation and commitment, like asking for monogamy and establishing a strong love language, isn't necessarily bad, it becomes an issue when unresolved traumas start to negatively impact their partner. It diminishes the partners sense of self-esteem and also deters us to what we truly want.

What to Do if You Suspect Predatory Behavior

Having clarified that, let's consider the appropriate course of action if you find yourself the target of predation.

It may be an instinct to immediately tell that person off and immediately dismiss them. This will disrupt your own peace. Your whole day could be riddled with anger and then you tell other people about it and disrupt their peace with something that may be easily dismissed with one simple phrase. When you are being preyed on and you are not enjoying the come-on, respond with one of the following:

- "Thank you for the compliment. Sorry, we aren't a match. Happy searching.
- "I appreciate the kind words. While I don't think we're compatible, good luck on your journey."
- "Thanks for the observation. I'm not seeing a connection, but best wishes to you."

These simple lines are incredibly impactful. They are carefully crafted to address many issues in the moment. I have the first one saved as a quick text. When I was on the apps and someone tried to message me, instead of ghosting or blocking them, I would reply with that if I was not interested or thought there wouldn't be a connection. Even in person, I have that line etched in my mind so I can readily use it whenever I need to. If someone compliments me and then tries to feel me up, I slide away, say the line, and walk away.

The first part in each line is a compliment. It can be a bit scary to make yourself vulnerable to say or express to someone else they are attractive. While your immediate instinct to a predator is to not consider their feelings and emotions, it is important for them and for yourself. For them, it gives them a sense of security in themselves that it is ok to compliment someone or show an appreciation toward another human being. If they don't think they can do that, they have potential to make the world an even uglier place. It builds resentment in them, and they can take it out on others or even more so, you. For yourself, it gives you a sense of joy knowing you did something nice for someone else even if their want doesn't align with yours.

The second part in each line is a definitive to shut the interaction down. It's defining your boundary and drawing the line of consent.

The third part in each line is saying, even though I am not interested, I'm sure you'll find someone else who is. I'm aware it's still giving the predator power to continue their search potentially attacking someone else. You don't have the right to teach them a lesson. Yet.

Nine times out of ten, people respect it and thank you for being clear with them. However, there are a few moments when they decide to challenge your response. Common reactions I have received in these circumstances include: "Why not?" "Come on, give me a chance." "You don't even know me; how could you dismiss me so quickly?" Or my favorite, "I can be very generous if you let me"

All these responses, while they may appear harmless, prioritize their needs over yours. If they don't respect the line and don't move on, that's when you can draw your claws out. Put on your defensive face because this is where things can get messy.

You are entitled to consider them as a predator at this moment. You possess every right to adopt a defensive stance because they have just demonstrated a disregard for your boundaries. By doing so, they devalue your desires and place their own needs and wants before yours. The decision of how to address the situation rests with you. There is no obligation to provide an immediate response.

When this happens, I tend to walk away or not respond to their answer. I like to leave them thinking about what they said and how it is wrong without having to say anything. Sometimes a non-response is a response in itself. Not responding is an indication of no and you don't want to engage further. You already gave them the respect with the rejection line, it's up to them to accept it.

If you choose to respond, be very careful. Replying could pull you into a situation where you waste your time and energy on someone you're not even interested in, leaving less room for someone you genuinely care about. Plus, you risk your privacy and wellbeing for someone who doesn't even matter to you. Why take such a risk? You're essentially responding for someone else's sake, not your own—so why bother when it's not really necessary?

Maybe you don't want to come across as rude, or you're thinking about how you'll probably run into them often and you'd rather avoid awkward situations. There are times when we just want to make others happy, and the idea of someone disliking us can really gnaw at us. We do this out of fear that they might push us away if we don't accept them, or because we feel an overwhelming need to be liked by everyone. But the truth is, there will always be some people who just don't like us, no matter what. It's crucial to make peace with this so you don't end up losing yourself. Maintaining your self-esteem and self-worth in these moments matters immensely, as it helps you stay confident and genuine, both with yourself and others.

Sometimes, people avoid confrontation by ghosting or making up excuses to escape from those who make them uncomfortable. This approach, however, can leave the other person stuck in their insecurities, struggling to understand what went wrong. They might start spinning tales about themselves—or worse, about you. Such situations might also give them a chance to come up with new ways to chase after you. It's crucial to address the issue swiftly before it spirals out of control and gets really messy.

However, it is their responsibility to act courteously, not yours to correct their behavior. When formulating your response, eschew excuses, ghosting, or deceit; instead, be completely genuine and clear. Anything less may lead to complications later, exposing you further to this unwanted person. I have prepared some responses to strengthen your position in case your initial reply is insufficient, and you choose to take this risk:

- "I don't have a romantic interest toward you."
- "I want things be strictly platonic between us."
- "I was giving you a respectful space to disengage, please respect my wants."

If these suggestions don't work and the person keeps bothering you, try not to be alone when you see them again. Make sure you have friends or acquaintances with you. It's also a good idea to tell others who this person is and what's going on. Look out for yourself, and let others look out for you too. If the problem is only happening through messages or on an app, block that person right away. At this stage, it's necessary. Even simple situations can turn into bigger problems if you're not careful, leaving you vulnerable. It's super important to protect yourself from these creeps.

PORNOGRAPHY

Addressing the subject of pornography might seem out of place when our goal is to empower our younger selves to overcome the challenges life presents and achieve our desires. However, pornography comes with inherent obstacles. It can erode a strong sense of self, foster unrealistic views and expectations, and introduce physical impacts. Yet, it can also serve as an educational resource, shedding light on the mechanics of sex, clarifying personal and partner preferences, and acting as a communication tool. Additionally, it has the potential to help set boundaries and bolster self-esteem or confidence.

Its creation and use spark much debate. Among teens and young adults, 90% and 96%, respectively, feel comfortable, accepting, or neutral when discussing porn with their friends. Meanwhile, 55% of adults aged 25 and over believe porn is wrong. For teens and young adults aged 13 to 23, not recycling is seen as a bigger issue than viewing pornography. Interestingly, 43% of teens and 31% of young adults think that porn is harmful to society.[19]

No matter where you stand on the issue of pornography, it's crucial to understand its strengths and weaknesses. By doing so, we can work towards becoming the best versions of ourselves, fostering deeper connections with others, and moving past our immature selves.

---

[19] Fradd, M. (2024, January 2). 10 Shocking Stats About Teens And Pornography. Retrieved from CovenantEyes: https://www.covenanteyes.com/blog/10-shocking-stats-about-teens-and-pornography/

Addiction

Pornography can be as addictive as substances like drugs and alcohol. Both activities trigger a surge of dopamine. Powerful drugs such as opioids, cocaine, and nicotine overwhelm the brain's reward system with extraordinary amounts of dopamine, ten times the levels produced by natural rewards. Similarly, pornography can be equally addictive, if not more so, due to its readily accessible and discreet nature on the internet. [20] Though porn addiction might not wreak physical havoc in the same way drugs do, it can undeniably have profound social repercussions.

The American Psychiatric Association does not officially classify addiction to pornography as a distinct diagnosis. Some professionals consider it under the broader category of hyper-sexual disorder, which can include behaviors such as excessive masturbation. Even if a therapist doesn't accept pornography addiction as an official diagnosis, researchers have developed various models identifying the signs associated with these behaviors. Some therapists hold the view that pornography itself is not inherently problematic but can become an issue depending on its impact on an individual and their relationships.

Researchers have found that pornography might be causing some serious problems in people's lives. These problems can show up as less satisfaction in their sex life, issues in their relationships, feeling less happy with their partner, or even taking risks to watch porn, like doing it at work.

If someone has an unhealthy relationship with porn, the signs might be clear. They might be ignoring their responsibilities just to watch it, needing to view increasingly extreme content to feel the same release that milder porn once provided, feeling frustrated or ashamed after watching but still not being able to stop, spending lots of money on porn instead

---

[20] Love T, Laier C, Brand M, Hatch L, Hajela R. Neuroscience of Internet Pornography Addiction: A Review and Update. Behav Sci (Basel). 2015 Sep 18;5(3):388-433. doi: 10.3390/bs5030388. PMID: 26393658; PMCID: PMC4600144.

of properly funding daily or family needs, and using it as a way to deal with sadness, anxiety, insomnia, or other mental health issues.

If you are uncertain whether porn is affecting your life, pause for a moment. Ask yourself some questions.

- Do you find yourself turning to porn as a way to escape your feelings or problems?
- Does trying to cut back on porn make you feel edgy or irritable?
- Are your thoughts frequently consumed by the urge to watch porn?
- Do you watch it and then wish you could stop, feeling a sense of shame?
- Have you ever lied to someone about how much you watch?
- Is it getting in the way of your social life, work, or hobbies?
- Do you often end up watching porn much longer than you planned?

Let's remember, just because someone watches porn doesn't automatically mean they're addicted. You might notice some of the signs I mentioned earlier, but ultimately it comes down to how it affects you personally. If you feel that watching porn is taking away from your life or harming your relationships, then it might be time to reconsider your habits. On the other hand, if you believe your relationship with porn is healthy, then by all means, 'have at it.' However, let's take a closer look at how porn can sometimes hold us young adults back.

Lose a strong sense of self

There's a world hidden in the depths of the internet that we often dive into without a second thought. Just a single search can whisk us away into countless unknown possibilities, leading us further from who we thought we were. It's so easy to lose track of our original intentions, caught in the thrall of endless fantasy. Sometimes, we share parts of ourselves online in ways our parents could never fathom.

Just as apps create a universal definition of what is acceptable and influence us to conform to societal norms, pornography does the same. It constructs various scenarios that we tend to accept as normal and defines what is sexually pleasing to others, often molding our ideologies to fit these narratives.

Porn sites may push boundaries to gain more clicks, and they're adept at identifying what is popular. These sites excel at marketing, drawing us into something potentially harmful. For example, porn sites increasingly use the terms "dad" and "daddy." Originally, this kink was categorized under the term "mature." In the 70s, gay porn showcased the "daddy" figure as an older man offering emotional and sexual guidance. Interestingly, a site like PornHub has found that 96% of women today search for "daddy" along with terms like "stepdaughter" and "daughter" remaining popular.[21]

The allure lies in these young women, often in their 20s, saying "daddy" in a high-pitched, innocent voice, highlighting the power and masculinity of the older figure. This trend, long prevalent in the gay community, is now being picked up by women—even as they continually fight for independence and power in daily life.

In the gay community, the "daddy" dynamic has always been a significant part of the culture. But what does that mean for us young men personally? Should we embrace it, or acknowledge it and move beyond it? If we adopt this role, we might be allowing men to retain power and masculinity. If we accept it, we might inadvertently be saying it's okay to take on a submissive role rather than striving for equality. Moving away from it means recognizing and embracing a different kind of power and masculinity within ourselves as young adults.

This shift can transform how we see ourselves. We might often see ourselves as the "boy" in these scenarios and seek out powerful figures in real life. We might think that emulating the younger guy in these situations will help us attract the powerful, attractive older guys we admire. However, stepping away from these narratives, we should realize that

---

[21] Pornhub. (2016). Who's Your Daddy? Retrieved from Pornhub Insights: https://www.pornhub.com/insights/daddys-dad

playing this part shouldn't dictate our actions or how we present our-selves. We shouldn't let these ideas shape our behavior or identity. Just as women who grapple with the "daddy" term still fight for independence and power, we too should strive for our own authenticity and strength.

Although data from PornHub indicates that a significant number of women searching for adult content are interested in 'daddy' porn, this doesn't mean that most women want to surrender all their power to men. In fact, a 2020 study by the Pew Research Center surveyed women across 34 countries and found that 94% believe women should have equal rights to men, with 74% considering it very important.[22] Remember how I mentioned earlier about apps: we can sometimes focus on a small segment and mistakenly assume their views are universal. Not all women watch porn, but the vast majority of women believe in equality with men. This desire for equality suggests that women don't want to give their power to men, but to be seen as equals and should be allowed the same rights and privileges. Some may believe in more rights and privileges, but that's a whole other debate and perhaps a different book.

OnlyFans

OnlyFans is a social media sharing platform with individuals and couples sharing their sexual experience with others online. The intent for the cre-ator is to generate interest and money tapping into the multi-billion-dollar pornography industry without signing up with a studio. They can upload anything risking being permanently scarred for life damaging their ca-reers and personal lives.

In this site, there are content creators and users. The content creators are creating the content while the user is viewing it. In 2024, the aver-age OnlyFans content creator is 29 years old and over 2 million content

[22] Juliana Horowitz, J. F. (2020, April 30). Worldwide Optimism About Future of Gender Equality, Even as Many See Advantages for Men. Washington, DC: Pew Research Center. Retrieved from Pew Research Center: https://www.pewresearch. org/social-trends/2020/04/30/worldwide-optimism-about-future-of-gender-equal-ity-even-as-many-see-advantages-for-men/

creators. The average monthly earning for a content creator is $180 with top earners earning above $100k a year. There are over 170 million users in 2024 with 500k new users daily. 90% of users are married.[23]

You might be surprised to learn that the average age of a content creator on OnlyFans is 29, and their typical monthly earnings are around $180. While some individuals pursue this path seeking sexual liberation or financial gain, they often find it's not worth the trouble. Many who leave this line of work do so because the objectification and degradation simply don't justify the paycheck. It can be unsettling when subscribers start pushing your boundaries, demanding more even when you're not comfortable. This platform can attract predators and stalkers, a reality you probably never expected to face. There's a real possibility that your name, location, and personal photos could be leaked. Not to mention that your content might get posted on other porn sites or social media channels, potentially exposing you to coworkers, family, and friends. These are some of the reasons why numerous content creators decide to quit or avoid joining OnlyFans at all.

Relationships

Porn just can't replace real intimacy. When you watch porn, you strip away the vulnerability that's essential for building trust and bonding in a genuine relationship. Porn turns the people in the videos and photos into flat, one-dimensional entities, lacking depth and emotion. If we want to cultivate deeper connections with ourselves and others, we need to embrace a richer, more multi-faceted mindset.

People often turn to porn as a substitute for genuine connection. It creates this illusion of intimacy that we find incredibly attractive. We can enjoy that dreamy screen persona, even if we can't replicate it in real life. Now, imagine you meet someone in real life who resembles that screen persona you've been privately admiring. What if, all of a sudden, you

[23] Daniel, C. (2023, December 29). OnlyFans Users and Revenue Statistics. Retrieved from SignHouse: https://usesignhouse.com/blog/onlyfans-users/

have immediate sexual thoughts and only see this person as an object? You end up in a scenario where you value only their physical appearance, overlooking the deeper person inside. How could you hope to build a real connection if you're fixated only on their physical traits?

Look, don't get me wrong I've been instantly drawn to someone because of their looks. That doesn't mean we should ignore someone's good appearance. For me, it's often about what those looks represent. For instance, someone with great teeth makes me think of good personal hygiene, which I find attractive. Or someone who dresses well signals to me that they care about their appearance and how others perceive them.

Other attractive qualities in a person could be their social circles or their relationship with their family. These traits go beyond physical appearance and delve into forming deeper connections with others.

When I think about porn, it's clear to me that it pushes the idea that objectifying others and being promiscuous is somehow acceptable. The actors on screen make it seem normal, even desirable. But deep down, I know that viewing people as mere objects and being promiscuous are completely at odds with forming genuine attachments. How can we truly connect and build bonds if we're just treating others as disposable? Real connections come from love, belonging, trust, and security, which seem impossible to achieve in the shadow of objectification and promiscuity.

Medical Impacts

Excessive porn use can really mess with your ability to have sex with someone, both emotionally and physically. Sometimes you might think the issue lies with your partner, but what if it's actually your porn habits?

Watching too much porn can lead to something known as porn-induced erectile dysfunction. If you find that you often need to think about porn to stay aroused during sex with your partner, it might make it hard to reach orgasm. This can be tied to watching porn frequently enough that it becomes a necessary component of your arousal process.

Another issue, sometimes called death grip syndrome, occurs when you're used to masturbating with a very firm grip. Although not a medically recognized condition, it refers to masturbation habits that make it challenging to achieve the same level of pleasure with a partner. This can lessen the sensitivity in your penis and might even lead to injury, anxiety, or depression.

When you can only ejaculate by thinking of porn scenes or using an overly tight grip, it can definitely create intimacy problems. Your partner might feel inadequate or develop insecurities. To build stronger relationships, it's worth looking at our own actions to see if they might be causing any tension.[24]

Benefits

Now that we've tackled the less appealing aspects of pornography, let's dive into some of its benefits. Pornography has been around for thousands of years, and for many young adults, it has become a significant source of sexual education. It covers topics that aren't usually discussed openly in school or among friends, thanks to its anonymous nature. By watching porn, individuals can learn about the mechanics of sex, discover what people find attractive, and figure out the positions or steps needed to please a partner. It can even serve as a communication tool in relationships, helping to set boundaries and boost self-esteem or confidence. It's essential to explore the nuances of porn and understand how it impacts our lives as young adults.

A survey of 425 OnlyFans users revealed some interesting insights. Only 8.7% of the respondents said they didn't learn anything new about sexual practices. Meanwhile, 28% used the platform to explore sexual orientation, and 20% to explore fetishes. The majority of users reported improved communication in their relationships, better boundaries, and

---

[24] Whittaker, G. (2020, December 27). Death Grip Syndrome: What It Is & How to Treat It. Retrieved from hims: https://www.hims.com/blog/death-grip-syndrome

increased self-esteem and confidence. Younger participants tended to learn more from the site.[25]

If you're new to sex or exploring a fetish that your partner is interested in, porn can be a useful tool to guide you through the basics and principles. It helps you understand whether something might be a turn-on for you. It can encourage communication between couples by providing a way to initiate conversations and discuss new experiences, adding an exciting dynamic to your intimate life. It offers guidance on how to broach new ideas and topics with each other.

If you're questioning your sexuality, porn can help you gauge your attraction to various genders without emotionally involving others while you figure things out. It's completely discreet, allowing you to gain confidence in your sexual preferences.

Sex is a significant source of dopamine, which can bring moments of joy, especially when dealing with negative emotions. While relying solely on porn may not be sustainable, it can provide a quick emotional boost. For instance, if you struggle to ejaculate with your partner and feel a drop in self-esteem because of it, porn can give you that ego boost and confidence, especially if you find it easier to reach orgasm.

How this impacts you?

A comprehensive study assessed university students in Poland, focusing on a sample of 1,135 individuals aged 18-26. Poland was selected for this research due to the unrestricted availability of adult pornography in the country. The findings revealed that 58.7% of participants felt that pornography use could negatively influence the quality of social relationships, 63.9% believed it affected mental health, 67.7% thought

---

[25] Lippmann M, Lawlor N, Leistner CE. Learning on OnlyFans: User Perspectives on Knowledge and Skills Acquired on the Platform. Sex Cult. 2023 Jan 9:1-21. doi: 10.1007/s12119-022-10060-0. Epub ahead of print. PMID: 36685612; PMCID: PMC9838472.

it impacted sexual performance, and 78.1% felt it adversely affected psychosocial development during childhood and adolescence.[26]

This study really hit home for us young adults, exploring the effects of porn on our lives. More than half of us felt that porn had a negative impact, putting strain on our relationships. It can end up replacing real intimacy with a partner, mess with our ability to connect on a deeper level, drag us into a harmful addiction that stands in the way of meaningful connections and a fulfilling life, and cause both physical and emotional pain. Plus, it can give us a distorted sense of who we are and how we relate to others.

If you think you might be addicted to porn or dealing with a type of erectile dysfunction known as a "death grip," it's really important to consider cutting back or even eliminating your porn usage. If you suspect it's an addiction, aim to go without porn for 90 days. This three-month period is crucial because it gives your brain the time it needs to reset.

Quitting porn can be really tough since your brain has been getting used to those dopamine highs, so it's essential to find other activities that bring you joy to fill that void. If you're struggling with being intimate or ejaculating with a partner but don't believe you're addicted, try abstaining from porn for just two weeks. This shorter detox can help restore sensitivity and allow you to appreciate your partner and the intimacy you share, rather than comparing it to the dreamy screen scenes.

This chapter isn't about pointing fingers at porn; it's about understanding the risks of letting it take the wheel of your life. Like being stuck in a bad relationship, it can cloud your mind and crowd out space for true, meaningful connections. By acknowledging the effects porn can have, we empower ourselves to handle it in a way that aligns with our personal needs, keeping control in our hands. This awareness helps us identify any barriers in forming deeper bonds with ourselves and those around us, giving us a chance to nurture a more confident and authentic self.

---

[26] Dwulit AD, Rzymski P. Prevalence, Patterns and Self-Perceived Effects of Pornography Consumption in Polish University Students: A Cross-Sectional Study. International Journal of Environmental Research and Public Health. 2019; 16(10):1861. https://doi.org/10.3390/ijerph16101861

TOXIC SITUATIONSHIPS

YOU ARE LOVED, UNTIL YOU ARE NOT.

So, have you ever found yourself in something that's definitely not a relationship but somehow, you're more than just friends? It's this confusing in-between space that's not quite black and white, you know? It's like you're committed, but not really, and your kind of just floating there without any real titles or clear hopes of what it should or shouldn't be. We might find ourselves engaged in a situationship, involved in an affair, or perhaps entangled in both scenarios.

In a world where love and relationships take myriad forms, the "situationship" has emerged as a modern romantic phenomenon. Coined by Cosmopolitan Magazine in 2017 amidst the surge of dating apps, this term describes a romantic or sexual bond that lacks formal definition.[27] In 2024, 39% of Americans have found themselves in such undefined territory, with that number rising to 50% among individuals aged 18 to 34.[28]

Growing up, it often feels like real relationships are this giant puzzle we haven't figured out yet. There's this sneaky voice in our heads telling us we're just kids playing at adulthood, clueless about love or the truths of life. And when that voice gets loud, whispering we're too green or just not ready for something serious, that's when we might start to ponder

---

[27] Hsieh, C. (2017, May 1). Is the "Situationship" Ruining Modern Romance? Retrieved from Cosmopolitan Magazine: https://www.cosmopolitan.com/sex-love/a9566889/what-is-a-situationship/

[28] Shah, K. (2024, January 31). Half of 18 to 34 aged Americans have been in a 'situationship'. Retrieved from YouGov: https://business.yougov.com/content/48492-half-of-18-to-34-aged-americans-have-been-in-a-situationship

whether dabbling in something more casual, like a situationship, could be our speed.

Can we be happy and healthy in a situationship? Many may disagree because of the lack of structure, but let's push back on this. Ask yourself if you can have love, support, a feeling of inclusion, and trust that satisfies your core need. If you can feel love and give love to its full capacity, generate support by others, feel good talking about your situationship with others, and trust each other to feel secure, then by all means. However, it is often difficult to achieve this in a situationship. There's still a lot of stigmas around it and the question remains, are we deserving of a situationship?

Let's go over the stigma around a situationship. There's still an overarching expectation from society that we should be married. Being married shows we are wholesome. It's seen as the happy ending. It allows the possibility for children to come home to a safe home. It shows you are grounded and committed. Whether this is actually true or not is beside the point, it's what many people believe.

Also, due to the ambiguous boundaries, it is commonly believed that individuals cannot find happiness or well-being in a situationship because navigating it is too challenging. It might appear that they do not merit these uncertain expectations and limitations. It is not akin to dating; rather, it is a stagnant relationship that fails to progress. People may criticize those in a situationship as being incapable of managing the responsibilities of a traditional relationship.

Hoping

If you're still hoping that your situationship will eventually become a full-fledged relationship, it might be time to face some hard truths. Situationships rarely grow into meaningful relationships. They often lack the emotional safety and the space for vulnerability that's essential for genuine intimacy. This is usually because there are no established steps for creating safety in a situationship since they don't have any defined boundaries or rules. Without these crucial elements, it's unlikely that you'll uncover the true potential of a relationship.

Remember when we discussed sexual vulnerabilities in the 'kinks and fetishes' chapter? We talked about Stephen Porges, PhD's theory on safety and vulnerability. When we don't feel safe, our survival mode kicks in, causing us to shut down to avoid connection, engagement, or offering the emotional warmth that healthy relationships need to flourish.

Think about your future. If you're picturing kids with your current situationship partner, you might need to think again. Or perhaps you're investing too much time and energy into someone who isn't serious about a committed relationship or children, leaving no room for someone who is. If there's an imbalance in your situationship, now could be the right time to step back and reassess where you're headed.

Waiting

If you're waiting for your almost-relationship to turn into something real, don't hold your breath. Situationships are a different kettle of fish compared to dating. With dating, there's an understanding that over time, as you spend more time together, it will evolve into a genuine relationship. Both people step into the dating arena with this in mind. There are steps and milestones in dating—like meeting for coffee first, then dinner, later perhaps having sex, meeting each other's friends, and setting boundaries. It's a journey that unfolds as you get to know each other and the relationship develops.

In a situationship, there aren't any clear rules or expectations, and you don't have to worry about what's coming next. The getting-to-know-you phase in a situationship is usually much shorter and often begins with physical intimacy. Diving into a physical relationship right off the bat can leave us feeling let down. There's just not enough time to build feelings of love, support, belonging, and trust with the other person. Starting at full throttle can leave us with nowhere to go. Rebuilding that intensity is incredibly challenging, and it might ruin any chance of making things work in the long run. If you think you've established a genuine connection with someone and then jump into bed on the first meeting, you're living in a fantasy. You've envisioned an ideal version of this person without really knowing if they meet your true needs. There's a reason why we take steps in dating before we become vulnerable in the bedroom and compromise our safety.

Believing

Love means choosing each other. If you or the other person are still keeping your options open, then neither of you has truly chosen to be together. Without a clear decision, there's always the risk that someone might find someone they like better. Or worse, you believe you're not worthy. Even if you think the other person is wonderful, without a definitive commitment, you're not on the same path as you would be in a traditional dating.

When you find yourself in a connection where you chose them, but they didn't choose you, you're clinging to a dream that they'll come around. From the start, they set up a situationship instead of moving toward a real relationship, showing they're not ready to commit. If you try to get closer, there's a good chance they'll withdraw.

If you believe it'll turn into a relationship, here's a test. Ask for what you want and provide an ultimatum.

Ultimatums/Boundaries

Let me share something from the heart. You know how ultimatums have gotten a bit of a bad rap, right? They're tagged as these unhealthy, unfair demands wrapped up in a do-or-die package. It's like dropping a bomb when someone tells you, "If you do this, you're going to regret it," and you can't help feeling cornered, maybe even a little on edge.

But, honestly, not all ultimatums are villains in disguise. We've all dished one out, maybe without even realizing it. Imagine you're telling someone, "Hey, that thing you did made me really uncomfortable, can we not go there again?" Or perhaps you're opening up, saying, "It stings a bit when you're texting your ex, do you mind being mindful of my feelings?" or even something as simple as, "I need a second to collect myself before we head out."

The key lies in how and when you say things. Think about it: if you give someone an ultimatum while you're angry, it often just escalates the situation, making it hard for either of you to really hear each other. Now, imagine the opposite scenario where you're both calm and genuinely listening. The respect between you is palpable. In that kind of atmosphere, gentle ultimatums can actually be quite effective. They're like vitamins for a relationship, giving it that little boost to keep things healthy.

Presenting an ultimatum or establishing boundaries in a situationship can be a healthy thing. Below are 4 scenarios where ultimatums and boundaries can help.

1. Not living in grey area anymore. If you are wanting a relationship with this person and not live in the grey area anymore, asking for what you want is very healthy. You may be surprised or disappointed but at least you are asking. It's a very powerful thing to know you want a relationship with this person and you should absolutely exude that power. An example of an ultimatum in this situation is, 'I really enjoy our time together, but I am looking for something with more substance. I need this moving toward a relationship that has two people committing to clearer boundaries and lines that I can boastfully talk to others about.' Or 'I don't feel good with how things are currently between us. I would like a real relationship with more defined rules, expectations, and the ability to easily explain to others what we are. I need this so I can feel better about the relationship we're in.'

2. Direction. If you or the other person isn't ready for a relationship but that is what you are wanting, perhaps asking to move the situationship into a dating relationship. An example of this can include, 'I don't feel our situationship is heading anywhere. I

want to explore a future with you and move this into a potential relationship. I want to move this situationship to us dating each other.' Another example is, 'What we have is great and I am really enjoying it. I feel this isn't going anywhere and I want to transition into dating each other so we can work toward a real relationship with each other.'

3. Feelings and emotions can be so tricky. So, what if you're feeling good in a situationship but you're also thinking about a real relationship with someone else? It's not like hooking up randomly, right? It doesn't seem like cheating if it's just a situationship anyway.

Now, throw a little jealousy into our already complicated situationship, and you're just asking for trouble. Trying to explain this mess to someone you're actually dating is like walking through a minefield—they probably won't understand, and honestly, who can blame them? It's a big turn-off. It makes me wonder; can we really give our best to someone who truly matters to us if our heart is tied up with someone else? Because, at the end of the day, love is about choosing to fully commit to each other, isn't it?

As highlighted in 'Situation Stigma,' less than 1% of couples are in open marriages. A 2020 study found that 20% of couples have tried consensual non-monogamy, but open marriages have a high 92% failure rate, with 80% of people in those marriages reporting jealousy. It's totally okay to admit that you're feeling jealous or that you don't want to risk feeling that way. You could say something like, "While I really enjoy this connection, I can't feel secure in this current dynamic and need it to feel better for myself and for you. Can we either end this or fully commit to each other?" This way, you're being honest about your feelings and protecting yourself from getting hurt.

If you're not feeling safe in this situationship, it's time to address it.

4. If you're dreaming of little feet pattering around the house, a situationship might not be the best route for you. It's really important to ensure you and your partner are on the same page about having children. If one of you isn't fully committed, it can create a mess of complications and worries about whether the child will receive the love and care they deserve. Just think about how a child might feel growing up in an unstable environment. It's heartbreaking to realize that kids from unsettled homes often struggle with feelings of darkness and inner turmoil, developing tough viewpoints on life. Of course, this isn't always the case, and life's unpredictable nature sometimes makes unconventional family structures necessary. Still, it's something that can weigh heavily on our hearts when we think about bringing a child into this world.

Addressing this could be as simple as asking your partner if they want to have children. If their answer doesn't match what you want, then it's time to end the situationship. But if you both want the same thing, then ask if they see this evolving into a stable relationship suitable for raising a child. You could say, "Our dreams for the future align, and we have a great connection. Do you see this turning into a stable relationship where a child would feel safe?" Usually, you won't need to explain what a 'safe' environment is for a child because people generally understand the social expectations of parenthood. But if needed, you can talk about how kids from broken homes sometimes miss out on experiencing true love and support because they never saw it growing up.

When A Situationship Turns Toxic

The people in a situationship aren't necessarily toxic, but the relationship itself can be. Below is a list of circumstances when a situationship turns toxic:

*   When it eats away at your own self-worth

- You start believing half-hearted love is all you're meant for
- Takes away from the things you deep down want
- Feelings of inferiority or a subordination
- It impacts other parts of your life (e.g. friendships, jobs, family)
- When they want to sleep with you, and your friends
- It's incredibly difficult to end

Let's break down each point and how each affects you should you find yourself in a toxic situationship.

Self-Worth

It's like you're giving them the power to judge whether you're worthy of something real, something whole. The very person who can't commit to you fully, you know? You let their hesitation sketch out who you are, what you'll become. Their hesitation becomes who you are. You may start believing that all people will be hesitant to be with you when the person you are in a situationship with and really enjoy, perhaps love, is showing you that you are not good enough to them for a full relationship. You're sharing more than a friendship with this person and being incredibly vulnerable when being physical with them. You value them and their opinion. You're spending a lot of time and energy with this person. It then manipulates you to have this skewed perception that others will think this too.

Slowly, you start to believe that maybe this half-hearted love is all you're meant for. You chip away at your own self-worth, your own plans for your life. What starts off seemingly harmless, just sneaks up on you and leaves you falling into this pit of self-doubt.

Half-Hearted Love

As you gradually chip away at your self-worth, you start to believe that this kind of half-hearted love is all you deserve. It feels like it's the only thing you can manage and the extent of what you're capable of. You could start to think that your love and energy should only go to those who won't fully invest in you. Over time, it begins to seem like you're only capable of this incomplete affection, doubting that you have what it takes to be in a genuine relationship.

Sometimes, we trick ourselves into thinking that situationships can teach us how to be in a real relationship. We might feel safer practicing our emotions with someone we know isn't going to be our long-term partner, hoping that when the right one comes along, we'll be ready. But we're fooling ourselves by practicing with someone who doesn't want a real commitment from us.

If you're in a situationship, chances are you're putting in effort and showing respect because it's more than just a casual fling. Ideally, these efforts are mutual. But if you're willing to give more and they're not, you're limiting your potential. You miss out on experiencing what it feels like to give your all to someone and have that love fully returned.

You find yourself unable to form deep connections with others because you've plunged into a state of self-doubt. You question if you're enough—good enough, giving enough, or even worthy enough. This uncertainty stems from being in a relationship where the other person is already maxed out in what they can give. They've reached their limit, while you're left yearning for more—more time, more energy, more commitment. In an effort to bridge that gap, you give more of yourself, only to be met with the same limited response. Sometimes, you might even start giving less, frustrated by the unchanging outcome. Eventually, even when you meet someone who's ready to offer a profound, genuine connection, you struggle to reciprocate fully. The past lack of reciprocation has left you unsure of how to truly express your love fearing rejection.

Takes Away from What You Want

If you're looking for a true relationship, it's incredibly challenging to juggle a situationship while also seeking out your special someone. You won't be giving your ideal partner a chance or space to enter your life if you're already investing your emotions, time, and energy in a situationship. We often immerse ourselves in these relationships because they feel good and go beyond a simple hookup. There's mutual respect, but as we pour more emotions, time, and energy into this person, we have less to offer someone who might align more with what we truly desire.

Moreover, being in a situationship when you're searching for a real relationship can lead this person to question your commitment. They might doubt your ability to fully love and give attention if they see you entertaining a situationship while looking elsewhere. It could appear that you're uncertain about what you truly want. This impression alone can be a deal-breaker, prompting them to seek someone more serious about a long-term relationship.

Inferiority/Subordinate

This feeling is particularly strong when you find yourself in a situationship with someone who is married or much older than you. If they are married, their spouse and their marriage take precedence over you. It's clear from the start that your position in their life is third and almost like you're filling a gap in their relationship. When the person is significantly older, it sends another hurtful message: they don't see you as good enough for a real relationship. Instead, they treat you like a 'kid,' not worthy of their full love and attention.

If they're married, it's unlikely you'll ever come close to ending their marriage. The pecking order is apparent: first comes their spouse, then their marriage, and then you. You're not valued as someone who could be in a committed relationship with them, and this reinforces a feeling of inferiority. They set all the rules, leaving you feeling subordinate because you are always their last consideration. It can be as simple as trying to see them on a particular date. They have to check their schedule and see if their partner has any plans for them. Only after that can they decide if they have time for you. If they were truly seeking someone else to be in a serious relationship with, they would have left their marriage already.

When the person is significantly older, the dynamic shifts in a way that makes you feel even more undervalued. They don't see you as an equal, treating you more like a child. You sense that you're not worthy of being in a serious relationship with them. If they saw that potential in you, they'd entertain the idea of something more substantial. However, in a situationship, they've already decided you don't meet their expectations. It may feel like age is a barrier, making you feel even younger and less adequate than you are.

Being in a subordinate role chip away at your sense of self-worth. You start doubting your own potential and begin to feel unworthy of being taken seriously or seen as a peer.

Impacts Other Parts of Your Life

Another thing to consider about situationships is how it can spill over into other areas of your life. When a situationship isn't fulfilling, we can get a little on edge, even with people who have nothing to do with it. We might get snippy at someone just because, at that moment, they remind us of not getting what we feel we need. It's like the frustration we feel with that person in the situationship starts to taint our friendships, job, and even the time spent with family. It's like when something's off in one corner of our heart, it's almost as though the rest of our life takes on the same shade of discontent.

Sleep With Your Friends

In situationships, there's often a hidden addiction to sex. You might find yourself with someone who flirts with your friends and anyone else they find attractive.

For younger people caught in these dynamics, friends or peers might react with disapproval. They could label this person as predatory, harboring strong negative feelings. They may see it as you being exploited, and they might not be entirely wrong. They could call this person a man-eater, someone who seduces and manipulates others for their own gain. They definitely wouldn't approve of someone like that taking up so much of your time and energy.

If someone said to you, "I want to sleep with you, and your friends," how would you react? Would you feel like your circle is being invaded? Would it risk your friendships because you're all being chased by the same person?

Maybe you start to feel like you're not special anymore, and you beat yourself up over it. You can begin to feel undervalued and unremarkable. And now, your group of friends is poisoned because you let this one person into your life.

Difficult To End

A situationship can often lead to developing deeper feelings for each other, but by definition, lacks the clear stages of a traditional relationship. It might initially begin with sex, followed by a reassessment to determine if there's more to connect on. What starts casually can evolve into something where we start doing more for one another and our feelings grow stronger. However, beginning casually makes it challenging to shift to a deeper, more meaningful relationship. It's tough to build a solid foundation when you start in the fast lane. As I mentioned before, starting quickly can leave us without direction. Trying to reignite that initial spark is very difficult and can jeopardize any chance of making things work long-term.

Without the natural progression that a traditional relationship has, we might find ourselves ending something that began at full speed. Ending a situationship that lasted three months can feel just as intense as ending a year-long relationship because of the heightened emotions and the lack of clear boundaries during those three months.

In a traditional relationship, there is an underlying expectation to keep it alive. Sometimes breaking it off can take time as there is a discover process and evaluation period. This can help emotionally handle a breakup should it occur in a real relationship as it's slowly putting out a flame. In a situationship, either party can abruptly break it off since there really isn't a commitment to each other. You can go from talking every day to suddenly being blocked and ghosted. This may be because one person is entering a real relationship with someone else and to keep the situation lingering can damage the new relationship. Or they don't feel accepted in the situationship and finally stood up for themselves to find more than what was being given.

The end of a situationship can also be difficult when there isn't as much support for the ending from friends and family. If they even know about the situationship, there isn't much sympathy considering it wasn't a real relationship. Your feelings are real but the expectations from the situationship didn't exist. Your support diminishes in these situations making it even harder to recover from than a real relationship.

If you find yourself stuck in a toxic situationship, it's likely because you're yearning for something more. It's completely natural to crave love, support, a sense of belonging, and trust. If this situationship isn't providing those things, it's time to let it go. You deserve to clear the space for someone who is ready and willing to offer you what you truly need. Your time, energy, and emotions are incredibly precious; don't waste them on someone who isn't committed to meeting your needs. Instead, focus on finding someone who wants to build a meaningful connection with you, where both of you can grow and thrive together.

PART TWO

TOXIC SIGNS

"SURRENDERING TO THE ILLUSION OF SOMEONE'S
GREATNESS, WHILE IGNORING THE POISON
THEY SLIP INTO YOUR LIFE, COMES AT A PRICE
TOO STEEP FOR YOUR HEART TO PAY."

Ahh...love. Love is an incredible feeling that pushes your boundaries and releases all kinds of intoxicating endorphins. It's an addictive dopamine. It can be totally blinding. Love is amazing, until it's not.

Have you ever felt that sinking feeling, like some people just want to tear you down, make you feel like you're worth less than you are? It's such an important thing, isn't it? To find those relationships where we're seen as equals instead of being stuck in some tug-of-war for power where we end up feeling small. Let's have a heart-to-heart about these toxic signs and figure out the best way to steer clear of them.

Let me give you an idea of what I do when looking for toxic signs. I do nothing. There's a certain comfort in nothing. I've done some of my best work on myself by doing nothing. I used to be so bad at reading people because I was investing so much work into relationships that I was distracted by my own work. Then I realized, in order to evaluate people, I simply had to do nothing.

People are naturally really good at showing you who they are. They don't even mean to. It's amazing how it just happens. People's actions and what they say are the only tools you need to read people. You can gauge their intentions, where they are in their growth, what kind of person they are and if they are capable of loving you.

I have crafted some of my favorite signs of what to look for and how to avoid them.

Mansplaining

As I mentioned before, I love working out. I know that doesn't sound like I like doing nothing but hear me out. I am at the gym every day. I made friends with the trainers, utilize various apps to change my routine, take classes, and have crafted my ideal body. You can say, I've been perfecting my art of working out and quite skilled at it.

I decide to bring a date to the gym. We both enjoy working out and it was our second date. I was showing him things and he was showing me things. We were learning from each other and having a blast. Halfway through the workout, he says to me, "if you want to really gain some serious muscle, you need to lift much heavier weights. I know you can do it, but you would look so much hotter if you lifted heavier weights."

Seems innocent right? What he said makes sense, but I don't lift heavy weights intentionally. I lift lower weights and go really slow for that time under tension. In this moment, I chose to say nothing and see where he was going with this.

He proceeds to grab some heavy weights and shows me a move. "See, this is how you should lift." He started lifting and then asked me to try. I did and was able to do it and looked at him confused. I had a better body than him, where is he going with this? He then proceeds to another workout grabbing another heavier weight that I don't normally lift. "Look at me closely and see how I lift this." He was sacrificing his form just to lift heavier too. Then I realized, this man is mansplaining me.

Mansplaining isn't a topic that's often talked about in the gay community because, by definition, it refers to a man condescendingly explaining something to a woman. But does mansplaining happen between men? Absolutely. Women tend to notice it quicker since it shows up more frequently when a man mansplains to a woman than to another man.

Three studies conducted at Michigan State University and Colorado State University explored this topic with 128 participants. They were observed during conversations about awarding bonus funds to deserving employees. The study found that women were less likely than men to want to work with a mansplainer again. They often experienced negative reactions, such as feeling uncomfortable and questioning their own competence. Women internalized negative feedback and felt incompetent after being talked down to by men. Even high-performing women sometimes opted out of opportunities to earn more money, choosing instead to avoid certain male coworkers due to the risk of mansplaining.

Men, on the other hand, reacted differently. They weren't as affected by condescending conversations or interruptions. The study suggested this might be because when men interrupt other men, it's often to say something positive like, "I agree," as opposed to the negative interruptions' women face. Just because we're not always tuned in to recognize signs of mansplaining, doesn't mean it doesn't exist. It's important to see it for what it is to protect our self-worth.[29]

I felt so lost and uncertain, questioning everything I thought I knew. There was a moment where I genuinely felt less than him, as though all the dedication I'd poured into working out was just wasted. I had to take a step back and remember all those hours of research and effort I've put into my fitness journey to regain my confidence. If I simply followed his advice and set aside my own knowledge, I'd end up completely dependent on him. It wouldn't just be about the workouts anymore; it would become a habit of not standing up for myself and always deferring to him. It's hard because I do want to see things from others' viewpoints, but I must keep reminding myself of the deep research and intense hard work behind my decisions to make sure I don't end up beholden to anybody.

People mansplain. Your family members can mansplain, the neighbor, coworkers, politicians, friends, and lovers. While seemingly innocent, can turn your relationship with that person to be controlling. Mansplaining doesn't have to come from men, but it stereotypically does. It's when someone explains something to you in a condescending way. It's unsolicited. They may not even realize they're doing it, but it is a toxic sign.

---

[29] Briggs CQ, Gardner DM, Ryan AM. Competence-Questioning Communication and Gender: Exploring Mansplaining, Ignoring, and Interruption Behaviors. J Bus Psychol. 2023 Jan 9:1-29. doi: 10.1007/s10869-022-09871-7. Epub ahead of print. PMID: 36686546; PMCID: PMC9838290.

Think about a time when someone was explaining something to you, and you were the expert in that topic, but you let them carry on. How did it make you feel? Did it make you feel inferior? Did it make you feel you were being talked down to? Did it trigger a past event? Remember, you are not a boy, and you don't need anyone to treat you as such.

When someone starts to mansplain, it might seem like a tiny, nagging issue, but let me tell you, it can chip away at your sense of value. They're pretty much waving a flag that says, "Hey, I think I've got the upper hand in knowledge here." Now, don't get me wrong, there are times when they actually do, and it's really a treat to learn something new. That said, when you're the one holding the torch of expertise in your hands, it's not just an opportunity - it's your moment under the spotlight. It's like watching a boy grow into his own, standing tall and speaking with a voice that resonates with confidence. When you step up like that, take the reins and gently put things straight, it's more than just a shift in the conversation. It's you living your truth and showing everyone that what you have to say is worth their attention.

Magnetic Charisma/Love Bombing

Imagine a different scenario: You encounter a person whose charisma is absolutely magnetic. Before you know it, they're showering you with affection and all kinds of gifts. They open up to you, confessing that you've become irreplaceable to them, that you're the missing puzzle piece in their life, and they do so with an intensity that takes you by surprise. You bask in this glory, feeling like you've found someone who recognizes your strengths and rewards you for your accomplishments. You feel incredibly positive about this person and begin to think that maybe you can't live without them.

Let me tell you about a practice called love bombing. It's a tactic where someone overwhelms you with intense attention and affection, but not out of genuine care. Instead, it's a way to manipulate you. At first, all the attention feels great, but it can soon lead to gaslighting and sometimes even abuse.

Love bombing usually happens in three stages: idealization, devaluation, and discard. Initially, they put you on a pedestal, making you feel incredibly special. But then things take a turn; they become cruel and abusive, especially when no one else is around. Finally, they discard you without taking any responsibility for the hurt they've caused.

A study involving 484 college students revealed a strong link between love bombing and traits like narcissism, insecure attachment, and low self-esteem.[30] It's interesting to note that millennials seem to exhibit more narcissistic tendencies than previous generations.

Love bombers are often very good at targeting vulnerable people, such as those who have just gone through a divorce, recently ended a relationship, or struggle with low self-esteem. In our experience, they often go after the young and seemingly vulnerable.

When you're deep into a relationship, love bombing seems more like a natural extension of your bond. But early on, it's a red flag. After all, how can someone truly know you in such a short time? Building a real connection takes patience and genuine effort. As you invest more time in each other, you start to understand one another more deeply. But if heaps of adoration come your way from the start, take a step back and really think about what's going on.

When someone showers you with presents and breathlessly claims they just can't imagine a life without you from the get-go, it's often not about you at all. It feels a bit like they're wearing a mask to cover up the cracks of their own self-doubt. Maybe they're leaning on you like a crutch, trying to find in you the validation they're missing within themselves. And when they're pulling you in, fast and furious, it might be more than affection—it could be a toxic sign, an attempt to dazzle you so you won't notice what's really lying beneath that glossy exterior.

---

[30] Strutzenberg, C. C., Wiersma-Mosley, J. D., Jozkowski, K. N., & Becnel, J. N. (2017). Love-bombing: A Narcissistic Approach to Relationship Formation. Discovery, The Student Journal of Dale Bumpers College of Agricultural, Food and Life Sciences, 18 (1), 81-89. Retrieved from https://scholarworks.uark.edu/discoverymag/vol18/iss1/14

Let's face it, we're still strangers to each other at the start. It's crucial to peel back the layers and understand the rush.

Imagine, just for a moment, what it would feel like if someone gazed into your eyes and somehow managed to peer straight into the essence of who you are. They have been adrift on a journey, searching high and low for the one who fits their soul like a missing puzzle piece. And in all their earnestness, they believe you are the one. It's a pure fantasy and why magnetic charisma is so effective.

I often wonder if certain things are truly possible, having been deceived multiple times. I vividly remember an encounter with a man named Barry. From our first meeting, Barry seemed inexplicably drawn to me. Despite being married, he showed a strong interest in me. He approached me, and though I politely turned him down because he was married and not someone I could see myself with, he persisted.

He showered me with questions, genuinely interested in everything I had to say. Our conversation lasted longer than I intended, as Barry kept drawing me back in, making me feel both flattered and understood. Amidst our talk, he confessed that he loved me, even though it was our first encounter, and I had just exited a relationship. Caught up in the moment and feeling good about the attention, I ended up spending the night with him.

However, once it was over, I felt discarded, his interest fading away swiftly. His attention resurfaced only when he wanted something from me on his own time, vanishing just as quickly when I no longer served a purpose for him.

I get so taken aback by someone's immediate affection and feel rewarded. It's rare to feel awarded especially when life always beats us down saying we aren't good enough, or worse, we say it to ourselves. I've also been that person who's always worn their heart on their sleeve, getting attached to someone at the drop of a hat when there's a bit of a spark. But, after getting hurt more times than I care to count, I've learned that those sparks, as alluring as they are, can sting you if you reach out too quickly.

When it comes to love, those with a lot to give tend to guard their hearts closely. They often find themselves overcompensating in relationships, always wary of being taken advantage of or feeling unappreciated. Such individuals are meticulous in choosing the right partner and take their time to assess whether someone is worth investing in. They dedicate energy to understanding people, ensuring their time is well spent. You and I are no different. We should take it slow at the start, truly get to know each other, and then, once we're certain that this connection is worth it, we can pump the accelerator once we are sure this person is worth it.

In this chapter of our lives, we're gently steering the ship of our relationships toward a more balanced horizon. Because the truth is, we're not on a quest for a love that shrinks our worth. We're no longer that young, eager soul who leaps without looking, only to find ourselves in the arms of someone who's thinking only of themselves, at our expense.

Unclear Intentions

This particular toxic sign is shown by asking early on what someone wants or perhaps, what we want. Unfortunately, the indication of this sign is when we must break free from doing nothing.

If you know what you want and someone else doesn't, it makes it hard to assess if this person deserves your time and energy. If they're not clear about their desires early on, it might indicate they struggle with decision-making in their own lives. It's not about deciding whether they want to be with you yet; it's about them knowing how they see themselves and their future. They might not be ready to decide if you're the right person for a relationship, but they should at least be able to communicate their goals and intentions. There's a necessary level of responsibility early on to decide what our intentions are.

I dislike the phrases 'go with the flow' or 'let things happen naturally.' While it's crucial to allow a relationship to develop naturally, these phrases can sometimes be an excuse to shirk responsibility. As children, we avoid responsibility and pass it to our parents. As adults, we must take on responsibilities and make decisions. Sometimes we avoid committing by saying we'll 'go with the flow,' but if you have intentions, they should be communicated. Not showing intent allows the other person to overlook your feelings and treat you dismissively, like a child.

If we spend time with people who aren't clear about what they want, we're being manipulated to fit their needs and desires, not valued for our time and energy. This is toxic because you might just be going along for a joy ride for their benefit, not yours. For instance, if you want a relationship and they don't, and they can't clearly express that, you're wasting your time and investing your emotions in someone who may not give you what you're looking for. They could also give you false hope and put you into a world of fantasy rather than reality.

We discussed three clear signs of toxicity: mansplaining, magnetic charisma/love bombing, and unclear intentions. All three of which can diminish your self-worth early in a relationship. Now, let's examine the indicators that someone is trying to devalue you if we perhaps ignored toxic signs in the beginning and got hurt after spending more time together.

Indicators that Someone is Trying to Devalue You

Consider that several months have elapsed and you find yourself deeply enjoying the rapport you've established with someone. You've went slow and haven't seen any major toxic signs. You've both decided that you want each other in your lives. It's time to pump the accelerator.

When we are accelerating, it's tough to see additional toxic signs. We tend to ignore them and keep driving. But there are signs on the road for a reason. Additional toxic signs that the person perceives you as less than an equal adult may include:

- ☐ Not prioritizing the relationship
- ☐ Coddling instead of caring
- ☐ Keeping the relationship secret
- ☐ I Am Not Your Boy 89
- ☐ Dismissing opinions

☐ Playing the victim
☐ Pressuring someone to change their personality

Not Prioritizing the Relationship

It's hard not to feel a little hurt when somebody isn't carving out moments for us. It leaves us wondering if they're actually into us at all. Maybe they're just swamped with other commitments, life has them in its grip. It's all too easy for any of us to get caught in the busy whirlwind and forget to pause for the simple joys. Still, we all find those fleeting escapes to brighten our days, like savoring that morning coffee that warms you from the inside. But, you know, if time keeps on slipping and we're not making each other a priority, it feels like we're not valuing each other enough. It's like saying we don't matter, and that sting doesn't go away easily.

When someone isn't carving out those moments, they are saying you are not a priority to them. This isn't always bad. Perhaps other priorities they have are good priorities and your place in the pecking order fits. Perhaps you like this person because of what they prioritize. But if they aren't prioritizing you to fill in their time with things you feel shouldn't go ahead of you, then it's a toxic sign.

An almost immediate reaction is to pressure this person to spend more time with you. We naturally do it as almost a primal instinct. We have needs and this person is not filling them, so we get angry and pressure them to do so. This comes in forms of making plans or telling this person to text you faster. But I'm here to tell you, resist that urge. Remember when I said I love doing nothing? In this case, this person is telling you they are putting you on the back burner. Let them. What should you do instead?

Advice:

Fill your time with things you want to do. Clean your place, work on a project, spend time with some friends. The important thing is to distract you from your phone and resist your urge to cling onto them. This allows a moment of missing each other and allowing them to come to you. If they truly want you, they'll make time for you. If you approach the situation this way, you'll feel better about yourself and better about the relationship. Allowing them to make time for you rather than you telling them to make time for you fosters a healthy equilibrium and restricts you from being perceived as nagging.

After giving them some time to miss you and stepping back a little, did they reach out to you? If they did, maybe that small distance worked. If they didn't, it might be worth considering if they genuinely want to be with you. In that case, take a moment to reflect on whether you want to stay in this relationship if you feel like they aren't valuing the relationship as much as you need them to.

Coddling Instead of Caring

Sometimes, you might feel wrapped in a bubble of supposed love and protection, and it can really seem sweet, like someone's giving you a warm, protective hug against the harshness of the world. But, you know, this might actually be someone shielding you from the stark truths and realities out there—almost as if they're whispering quietly that you might not have what it takes to face life's tough stuff head-on.

It's noticeable when they're glossing over the truths, not daring to give it to you straight, perhaps worried about how you might take it. They're the ones grabbing the wheel when a challenge looms on the horizon, stepping in before you even have a chance to show you can handle it solo.

Caring and coddling—though they might dress alike—they're not twins. Caring is all about supporting each other in a way that leaves everyone feeling heard, understood, and ready to take on the world. Coddling, that's a whole different story; it's like taking a detour around the hard stuff, no confrontation, no growth.

Imagine you're with someone who always takes charge of making plans while you just go along with the flow. They end up organizing everything, and you simply say yes or no. Maybe you do this because you don't feel confident about planning outings, or you think they don't trust you to organize a well thought out plan. It might seem like they're just filling in the gaps in the relationship, but essentially, they're pampering you. Instead of encouraging you to come up with plans or see what it's like for you to arrange a date night, they handle it all without even offering a guiding hand. Even if you think you're not great at making plans, know that it requires practice and genuine interest to improve. Having both people plan things is great for showing interest in the relationship and expressing your individuality. If they are such a great planner, learn from them and try it for yourself. That way it can go from coddling to caring.

This might seem like a minor issue, but these signs often snowball into more significant problems. When someone starts taking over parts of the relationship because they don't think you can handle things, it doesn't stop there. They might start making big decisions for you too, like buying a house, choosing where to live, and ultimately deciding what's best for you. That's when we lose control and get pushed into a submissive role, dependent on the other person.

Advice:

If you find you are being coddled, ask them why they don't allow you the opportunity to grow in that area? If they still don't let you grow in that particular area, question if this is going to be the dynamic of the entire relationship where you just fall privy to them rather than showcase your strengths. If they turn to be open minded and give you opportunities to grow, then take that opportunity to strengthen the bond.

If you're finding yourself in a place where real, heart-to-heart conversations just can't take root, you've got to wonder—are you being coddled instead of cared for? And where honest talk can't thrive, secrets tend to sprout like weeds. If there is no way of respectfully communicating situations like this, then perhaps you're already being controlled.

Keeping The Relationship Secret

When someone indicates to you that your relationship needs to be secret or you shouldn't talk about your feelings about the relationship to others, proceed with extreme caution. I've met some amazing masterminds in this art. I've had people take me to places where they wouldn't run into anyone they knew and justified it as wanting to spend quality alone time with me. I've run across situations where I was convinced, I shouldn't talk about my feelings with others and to only work with them on our feelings. That the relationship isn't a community project but a sole task. These are toxic and will diminish you as a person.

One thing we know about secrets is that they're designed to protect ourselves from outsider feelings and judgements. But what is so embarrassing about you? Don't answer that because there is no correct answer except for 'nothing.' If you feel you are being hidden, things aren't being as transparent as they should be. It could be many reasons why. Don't assume what they are. Ask with calmness and politeness and see their reaction. **If they get angry and defensive, they are lying about something**. It is a classic sign of someone lying and something incredibly important for us to remember. When people respond openly and want to hear more, they are inquiring how they can be better. They are validating your feelings. People who are truthful don't respond defensively.

If you are being trapped in silence from sharing your feelings from others, it's a sign of abuse. What they are really saying is, 'if you talk to your friends about us, they'll tell you to walk away from me.' This may come from a version of insecurity but more often than not it's because they know they are not treating you well. If they are knowingly not treating you well and still entertaining you, it's showing you inequity.

Advice:

If you feel enough time and emotions have passed where you shouldn't be kept secret, then you have every right to ask for openness to keep your self-worth. If you don't, you're telling this person you're accepting of the secrecy allowing them to test restricting you even more. If they feel not enough time and emotions have passed, listen to why. This could be a learning opportunity for you. Perhaps you're more open about things than they are and recognizing differences and respecting them is important. But if things remain to be secret, you can ask when things can become more public. Hold them accountable to a timeline because you are now doing them a favor and reducing your self-worth as a cost to that favor.

When you start feeling like you're always tucked away in secrecy, take a moment to ask yourself if you deserve to be in a relationship where there isn't a sense of belonging. Also, consider if the reason for hiding the relationship is because they're treating you poorly, and they're afraid others will advise you to leave. It's time to reassess your situation before things deteriorate further.

Dismissing Opinions

It's like you can just feel it when someone isn't taking you seriously, right? You'll catch them rolling their eyes whenever you put your two cents in. Or worse, they laugh, not because what you said was funny, but because they don't think it's worth a serious thought. You try to talk about something important, and they won't even give you the courtesy of looking you in the eye. Or you'll be midway through sharing your thoughts, and they just walk off, or give you this indifferent shrug, as if whatever you're saying is the least important thing in the world. It's pretty disheartening when that happens.

One of the clearest signs of this is when you are emotional and attempt to convey your feelings to them, yet they dismiss your words. They have a preference for positive feedback and may perceive you as being overly dramatic or emotional. Subsequently, they cease communication, anticipating that you will regain composure and offer an apology. When really more often than not it is them that is supposed to apologize. This behavior implicitly communicates their lack of serious consideration for your perspective and their unwillingness to be disturbed by any perceived negativity. This only serves to exacerbate your frustration because your attempts to be heard are not only disregarded but actively hindered. If someone is cherry-picking only the positive aspects and avoiding the tough parts, it indicates that your relationship with them is quite challenging.

These are classic signs this person is not taking you seriously. This is the perfect opportunity to pause and read the situation. Why is this happening? You have to wonder, haven't you been around long enough for your thoughts to matter? Is it possible they're so full of themselves they can't admit when they're wrong? Could it be they're just dodging any kind of tough talk or choices to sidestep accountability?

Sometimes it feels like they think they're on top, doesn't it? Like they've got the upper hand in our relationship. I've learned that it's up to us to shift that balance. I used to keep quiet to avoid disagreements. I remember being in a relationship with someone for two years. After the first year, I noticed he would openly flirt with others in front of me. He even texted others in a flirtatious manner. It really bothered me because he used the same flirtatious lines he would use with me. I never confronted him about it and just ignored his actions. I realized I was letting my feelings get trampled. Of course, I've also noticed that confronting someone in the heat of the moment is not the most effective approach.

Advice:

Take a beat to process what's gone down.

Take a quiet moment to sit down and read what's on your mind and the situation. It gives a chance to see things more clearly. When we thoughtfully express ourselves like that, we end up feeling more solid and heard. After a short time has passed, bring up the situation where you felt dismissed. See how they respond. If they think about it seriously and want to improve, listen to how they plan to move forward and hold them accountable.

If you still feel your opinions being dismissed, it may be time to re-evaluate the situation you're in. Ask yourself if this is just a one-time thing or if it's a pattern that's slowly chipping away at the trust and happiness you share with someone. It's tough but taking that hard look might help you figure out if there's a future where your voice is truly heard.

Playing The Victim

Have you ever told someone they were doing something wrong, only for them to immediately act like the victim? It can feel like gaslighting, where they turn it around and make you the bad guy instead of accepting responsibility. It happens over and over—every time you confront them, they flip the script on you. Even if they're not entirely at fault and we've misjudged the situation, they should still be open to the possibility of being wrong and willing to own up to it.

When it feels like the signs are pointing away from them being the one at fault, I can't help but end up a bit puzzled. It's like I'm suddenly the one who's been wronged, and I'm left scratching my head, wondering how the tables turned on me. Does this mix-up happen to you a lot when problems crop up?

Chances are, you aren't the one at fault. We test out the scenario by talking to our friends with our side of the story which may contain biases making it difficult to determine fault. However, if it continuously happens, it may not be you at all. It may be them using it as a coping mechanism to deal with tough situations. This coping mechanism comes from previous traumas or their own reluctance to accept accountability due to personal insecurities.

How does that impact the relationship or you? Well, you're left scared to make any moves in the relationship. You're being controlled and dominated to not have an equal place in the relationship. You destroy your own self-esteem and respect because you're being told from the person you value that you are always at fault. It allows them control and dominance over the relationship setting the dynamic to always work in their favor.

Advice:

Don't let them constantly play the victim, as doing so is a disservice to them. They might struggle to form lasting connections with others. This can make it difficult for them to open up, genuinely feel for other people, and it may even encourage them to continue this behavior. Deny responsibility and provide examples of how they are wrong. Present scenarios asking how they would feel if they were in your shoes.

Now, if someone's obviously at fault but they won't own up to it, it's worth taking a moment to consider whether this person is even capable of being in a deep, meaningful relationship. If it turns out they're not, it might be time to adjust what you expect from them, or maybe it's a sign that you should think about where the relationship is headed.

Pressuring Someone to Change Their Personality

If you are receiving pressure to change certain personality traits of yours, carefully evaluate the situation. It's not necessarily toxic if what they're asking you to change will strengthen the relationship. It is toxic when what they're asking you to change will alter who you are as a person.

A personality shift, which is toxic, comprises changing an individual's interests, motivations, values, self-perception, abilities, and emotional tendencies.

A strengthen the relationship shift, which is not necessarily toxic, can include demonstrations of affection, the exercise of compassion, the exhibition of respect, the display of consideration, and the allocation of time.

Here are some examples for you to think about and decide whether each scenario is a toxic personality shift or a non-toxic relationship strengthener:

- I don't want you hanging out with that group of friends

- I need you to be monogamous
- Will you skip your regular routine of Church on Sunday to hang out with me?
- I need you to be more public about this relationship
- I want you to quit smoking/drinking
- Will you lose weight so we can have better sex?
- Can you dress better, so I don't feel embarrassed by you?

Answer Key:
Toxic personality shifts:

- I don't want you hanging out with that group of friends
- I want you to quit smoking/drinking
- Will you lose weight so we can have better sex
- Can you dress better, so I don't feel embarrassed by you

Non-toxic relationship strengtheners:

- I need you to be monogamous
- Will you skip your regular routine of Church on Sunday to hang out with me?
- I need you to be more public about this relationship

How'd you do? When you notice someone trying to alter your personality, it might be because they're not truly drawn to who you are or perhaps, they struggle to step outside their own needs to build a healthy relationship. These could be indications that they're simply not ready to let someone else into their life. Maybe being single would suit them better.

Advice:

Stand your ground and be a little protective of yourself. Share what matters to you so they can understand why those things should matter to them as well. It's important to defend your individuality. If they conclude that who you are doesn't align with what they want in a relationship, it's perfectly fine to part ways. Remember, you shouldn't have to lose yourself for someone else; you deserve to maintain your own identity and not just become who they want you to be.

When reaching out for a little bit of understanding or help, it's always a good idea to come from a place of kindness and keep a level head. I find it helps to gently share with them the reasons behind your ask—it makes things clearer. But let's never forget that we're both human, and it's totally okay to voice what we need to nurture a deeper bond between us.

Conclusion

The signs are all there, etched painfully into every encounter. There's the dismissive tone that undermines our intelligence, the overwhelming affection that feels more manipulative than genuine, and the reckless decisions made without a second thought to their impact. Our needs are ignored, sidelined by misplaced priorities. Genuine care is replaced by patronizing gestures, and the sharp sting of hidden truths cuts deeper each time. Worst of all, there's a gaping hole where open, honest emotional exchange should be, leaving us feeling more alone than ever despite being together.

When we ignore these toxic signs, it's like we are feeding into a harmful cycle. We become part of the problem because we let it slide, and things just tend to spiral from bad to worse. That's the exact moment we need to rise up from inaction and start taking action.

It's from this new vantage point that we can choose our next steps with intention—whether to mend the ties or to part ways with grace. By nurturing this keen eye and fortitude, we slowly but surely filter out the toxicity.

RE-DEFINING PARENTAL CARE

ARE YOU BEING CARED FOR, OR CODDLED?

When you become a parent for the first time, there's a tendency to strive for perfection. The urge to be the best mom or dad—to shower your child with all the love, care, and support you can muster—can be overwhelming. Every tiny detail seems monumental, and you constantly worry about getting everything just right. Your baby becomes the focal point of your universe, demanding all your attention and energy. In this all-consuming dedication, however, it's easy to forget the importance of nurturing your relationship with your partner. Balancing the roles of parent and partner is no small feat.

As kids, we often see our parents' perfectionism and anxieties as expressions of their love and support. This becomes our baseline for what love means. We may not pay much attention to our parents' relationship because they focus so intently on us. Their devotion to us shapes our understanding of love, care, and security.

For more experienced parents, or those with multiple children, the experience shifts. The rigorous pursuit of perfection wanes as they settle for doing their best within more practical limits, learning from past mistakes to navigate a smoother parenting journey. While their primary focus remains on their children, their relationship often still takes a back seat.

Children of experienced parents may feel either neglected or more cared for, depending on how their parents adapted from their earlier experiences. Dynamics change further with siblings, introducing competition for attention and affection. These children may find themselves striving for reassurance, hoping to feel the same love and security that make them feel valued.

As we grow up, our sense of love, care, and support largely stems from how our parents treat us. Their relationship with each other often remains in the background because, as children, we aren't focused on them. Perhaps it's also because their energy is directed toward loving us. When we become adults and start navigating relationships, we use our parents' care for us as a model for what to seek in a partner. We tend to overlook the significance of their relationship with each other as a blueprint for a healthy partnership.

We often overlook a crucial aspect when seeking our own partners—understanding what made our parents' relationship work, rather than solely focusing on how they treated us. Whether our parents' relationship was good or bad, we tend to forget its dynamics as we search for our own soulmate. Sometimes, we get caught up in chasing the love, care, and support our parents provided us, rather than looking for the elements that actually made their relationship successful. When we search for parental love, care, and support, we risk becoming overly dependent. However, if we try to learn instead from the love our parents had for each other, we nurture healthier relationships with ourselves and with others.

And for you parents out there, think of this as a little tip for the journey. Sometimes, rather than zeroing in solely on the nitty-gritty of childcare, it might be worth considering the power of your own relationship as an example. By showing your children what a loving, healthy partnership looks like, you can set the stage for them to build strong, fulfilling connections for their future.

Overprotection

Every one of us has a unique narrative when it comes to family. Some of us grew up with parents who were our confidants, our closest friends, the anchors in our sea of emotions. We shared everything with them, and they knew us inside out. For others, the relationship was more detached, with emotions left unspoken and daily happenings kept private. No matter the specifics, our parents were our protectors. It was their job to keep us safe.

Sometimes, our parents' protectiveness felt stifling. They believed we weren't ready to grasp the essential skills needed for adulthood, so they stepped in and took charge. Their intentions were rooted in love, aimed at equipping us with the tools for success. Yet often we didn't get to voice our opinions on what was best for us because their fear of our failure led them to take over.

This dynamic fostered a certain reliance on our parents. We often turned to them for formidable decisions because that's what we were used to—they always had the final say. They guided us, but through the lens of their experiences and priorities. Consequently, making tough choices independently became a challenge, as we grew accustomed to their direction.

As we move into adulthood, the ever-present, nurturing parent might no longer be there. Suddenly, we are left with the responsibility of making those difficult decisions ourselves. The question lingers—are we prepared to take on this role? Can we trust our own judgment and abilities to navigate this world?

Search For Our Caretaker

When we grow up, it can be quite intimidating because we must now make our own decisions instead of relying on our parents to make them for us. Our parents once had the responsibility to provide love, care, and support, but now we must seek these things for ourselves. Sometimes, rather than accepting this responsibility, we delegate it to someone else. We might choose another person to be our caretaker in place of our parents. This happens because we sometimes doubt our own ability to take on this role.

When we assign someone to take care of us, we are relinquishing control and our destiny to someone else. They are calling the shots on how we should be living and making decisions for us. We are putting ourselves in a boy's shoes and not growing or living up to our full potential. We are limiting ourselves to have deeper meaningful connections.

Why do we believe we can't do it? Often, overprotective parents made decisions for us, leaving us with little autonomy. We didn't learn or grow by making our own choices; we merely followed orders. Over time, we might become complacent, allowing others to take charge because we grow lazy or perhaps because it feels like a relief after having to take care of ourselves for a long time. Though this reliance can seem appealing, it can become harmful when we turn a partner into a lifelong caretaker.

Instead of looking for a caretaker, we should seek someone who supports us and whom we can support in return. Navigating this life alone is almost impossible. While we can be remarkably independent and self-sufficient, there is a humbling sense of gratitude in asking others for help and depending on them. We need to be open to receiving care and advice from others to truly thrive. Seeking help can be daunting because it might make us feel insignificant, but in reality, utilizing all available insights and support makes us stronger and more capable.

So, how can we tell the difference between a caretaker and a supportive, loving partner? Ask yourself whether you are assigning someone to take care of you or allowing someone to care for you.

Care or Coddling?

You might find this a bit reminiscent of a part in "Toxic Signs." Here, we're delving into the subtle differences between growing up as your parents' child and recognizing coddling and caring tendencies versus looking for toxic signs in others.

Our parents, often with the best intentions, can unintentionally shield us too much, leaving us unready to face life on our own. To become truly self-reliant, it's important to identify the overprotective behaviors we've internalized and transform them into nurturing self-care practices. These coddling habits can resurface in our adult lives, so we need to consciously shift them to more supportive tendencies. Let's explore how we can spot these familiar parental protection techniques in our adult lives and turn them into healthy, caring habits. Growing up is about transitioning from being a dependent child to an independent adult, and in the process, creating our own foundations of security.

Coddling		**Caring**
Trackers	➡	Boundaries
Defines your environment	➡	Recreates a mutual environment
Determines what is 'healthy'	➡	Defines for ourselves what is healthy

Trackers vs Boundaries

Parents typically ask their child to report everything they've done to verify if it's appropriate to them. This could be as simple as asking where they were throughout the day. We often tell our parents as a means of being a good child and catering to their desires.

In many cases, this asks takes a step forward. With modern day technology, parents often employ actual trackers for their children. It is not uncommon these days for parents to install tracking applications on the mobile devices of their children as a method to always ensure their safety. This practice stems from a parental desire to confirm that their child is secure from potential dangers and are present at expected locations. This strategy is recognized as a precautionary measure exercised by guardians for the protection of minors under their care.

Conversely, the dynamics shift when you are being monitoring as an adult. Allowing someone else the ability to track you is assigning someone to take care of you. It is different from parental safeguards and veers into the realm of controlling conduct. In relationships devoid of power struggles or issues of trust, employing tracking devices voids the mutual understanding. Trust can be damaged when using trackers. Trust is a right that is earned and fostered.

Should there exist an imperative need for tracking, it is advisable to establish explicit limitations surrounding its usage. As an example, allowing location tracking may be considered reasonable when venturing into a dangerous area—permitting such monitoring exclusively for the duration within said territory or during specific intervals of the day. The emphasis must lie on minimal usage, thereby facilitating a supportive role for the tracker rather than always granting them an all-encompassing surveillance over one's whereabouts. Minimum use is seen as a supportive role where all access on your location is assigning them to take care of you.

As a rule of thumb, tasks that were imposed upon you during childhood by your parents are unlikely to be expectations you would impose upon another adult. If this is the case, it more accurately reflects a scenario where you are assigning someone the role of caretaker, rather than entering into a mutual arrangement where care is willingly provided.

A healthy transition from tracking tendencies is setting boundaries. Boundaries are typically established by parents for their children as a means of protection. These boundaries can include prohibitions on swearing, regulations pertaining to the amount of time spent with technology, or the establishment of expectations regarding responsibilities such as household chores. We are entrusting our parents with this duty and adhering to their guidelines.

You wouldn't assign these kinds of boundaries as an adult. Boundaries are a harsh word which almost sounds like there's a wall being placed in-between. But boundaries serve a purpose. It promotes independence, minimizes tendencies of codependence, and fosters the feelings of empowerment and respect. It also contributes to both emotional and physical comfort. It may seem seemingly harmless to not have boundaries with someone else, but it can attribute to control and trust issues. It can also lower someone's self-esteem as they become reliant on the other person to take care of them. Empowering each other with boundaries means allowing that person to have boundaries. For example, if you are struggling with a disability, you should be able to vocalize and explain the disability. If you allow someone else to speak for you as an attempt to shield you from explaining, you are doing yourself a disservice. You are relying on them rather than addressing the issue on your own.

Defined Environment vs Mutual Environment

Our parents, during our upbringing, decided where we would live, who we would be around, and the nature of our upbringing. They took care of us, and we trusted them to make decisions on our behalf. We hoped they would create a safe environment, providing a proper home, a loving and caring community, and the necessary tools for us to become successful, happy adults. This often reduced the stress and conflict we may have experienced with our parents.

In a study involving around 9,000 young adults, researchers aimed to discover the percentage who eventually left their parents' homes. By the age of 27, about 90% had taken this significant step, with the median age for moving out being 19.[31] This transition represents much more than just a change of address; it marks a profound journey toward personal growth. Gaining independence from our childhood home builds a stronger sense of confidence and self-esteem. Often, the new environment is calmer and less fraught with conflict, which can greatly benefit our mental health by reducing stress and tension.

Living on our own also teaches us invaluable life skills, fostering a sense of competence and self-reliance. It creates opportunities to form new social connections, enriching our lives and contributing positively to both physical and mental well-being.

Conversely, staying in our parents' home can present challenges. The lack of privacy can blur the boundaries necessary for personal growth. This situation might hinder our journey to independence, leaving us feeling less competent and self-reliant. Additionally, remaining in the family

---

[31] U.S. Bureau Of Labor Statistics. (2014, December). Independence for young millennials: moving out and boomeranging back. Retrieved from U.S. Bureau Of Labor Statistics: https://www.bls.gov/opub/mlr/2014/article/independence-for-young-millennials-moving-out-and-boomeranging-back.htm

home often leads to heightened stress and a sense of being trapped, impacting our overall sense of fulfillment and freedom.

One of the most liberating aspects of moving out is the newfound ability to chart your own course and shape your own lifestyle. Often, we unwittingly surrender our autonomy, letting others steer our decisions and lives, sometimes for a cherished partner or close friend. While these sacrifices can be acts of love, they must come from our genuine desires. Otherwise, we yield our power to others and avoid responsibility for our own choices. This can result in consequences similar to those experienced when returning to live with our parents, where they continue to make decisions for us. In such situations, establishing boundaries can be difficult, and we may feel less independent, competent, and self-reliant.

Navigating the complexities of such a decision requires deep consideration of its impact on both parties. Imagine Bill, someone you've come to love, invites you to move into his beautiful house in a desirable neighborhood. Currently, you live in a small apartment in a less favorable area due to financial constraints. Moving into Bill's home seems like the perfect chance to embrace a better living situation and realize your dream of living in a nice house.

However, it's important to consider the nuances of this transition. When you move into Bill's house, you're stepping into his world—his home, his community, his routines. This shift could impact your independence and well-being as you adapt to a lifestyle crafted by someone else. Instead of simply moving in with Bill, consider finding a new place together, one that you both select and cherish.

Choosing a shared home allows you both to create a mutually supportive environment. It enables each person to retain their essential life skills, confidence, and self-sufficiency. Moreover, it provides an excellent opportunity to cultivate new friendships and enrich your social circle, thereby contributing positively to your physical and mental health. By creating a home together, you can avoid potential feelings of obligation or confinement, fostering a space where both individuals can thrive and set healthy boundaries.

What's Healthy?

It is a parent's responsibility to instill healthy habits in their child when you're growing up. These habits encompass avoiding junk food, maintaining a good sleep pattern, showing interest in schoolwork, listening to elders, being kind to others, and possessing aspirations. The hope is that these habits will endure into adulthood, empowering you to make such decisions independently.

You get to decide as an adult what you deem as healthy. If you allow someone else to decide for you what is healthy, you're assigning the responsibility onto them. An example is forcing someone to eat healthy things. You're at a restaurant and you want fries alongside your burger. The person opposite of you tells the waiter that you will have the salad instead. You comply because it seems like this person has good intent and is watching out for you. But, if you want fries, get the fries.

Parents often tell you what to do as a child. You have to go to school. You have to get good grades. You have to pursue successful career choices. As an adult, we get to decide what we want. You're assigning the task if you have someone else decide for you what your life entails. A very popular example is if a male tells their female partner they want them to be a stay-at-home mother. It's one thing if the female wants to be a stay-at home-mother, it's another thing when the male assigns that task to the female.

Sharing the care. While growing up, one looks to one's parents for security. As adults, the responsibility for mutual safety is shared. This shared responsibility bestows a sense of empowerment on all parties, rather than consolidating power in a single individual. Engaging in acts of kindness towards others, and receiving such gestures in return, instills a feeling of contentment. By equally distributing the nurturing roles, we allow for reciprocal caretaking, thereby fostering a more equitable dynamic. Should one choose to be vulnerable, it is only fair that the other party be willing to express vulnerability as well.

Breaking Away to See Ourselves

Once we step out of our parents' shadows, it's our turn to tend to our own needs. Even after we've moved on, it's worth noting if you find yourself seeking that same kind of parental care in a partner. It's absolutely fine to ask for help and support, but when it's given without our request, that's when we need to tread carefully. It might seem harmless. We discussed numerous instances where responsibilities can be foisted upon us without us asking. The situation changes when we do ask for that help. When we don't seek it, we risk losing our sense of self, our individuality, and the core of our identity, reducing ourselves to dependents instead of acknowledging our growth and maturity.

How simple is it for you to succumb to the habit of entrusting another with caregiving responsibilities? It is, surprisingly, quite straightforward, particularly if you perceive yourself in a childlike manner. We frequently lack the self-assurance to advocate for ourselves, instead allowing others to assume control. We are so readily carried away, often looking to another to endow them with our trust entirely. Yet, what detrimental effects might this have on you?

It may now be apparent that such behavior leads to a loss of control over your destiny, a diminished sense of self or individuality, and the failure to realize your full potential. However, the recurrent act of falling into this snare constrains our capacity to forge profound and meaningful relationships.

By bringing your complete self, encompassing both your imperfections and strengths to the table, you foster a deeper connection with others. Molding your identity to meet another's expectations is a departure from authenticity. As children, we naturally adapted to our parents' standards, depending on their wisdom and care for our protection. However, as adults, we are endowed with the autonomy to make our own choices, and our parents can only hope that their upbringing has equipped us to make wise decisions. The groundwork has been laid for you. Although it may not always be of the highest quality, it is your responsibility to forge your own destiny. Failing to do so means falling short of realizing your true potential and the full breadth of who you are.

When individuals are subjected to the influence of another's control, they implicitly signal to the world their vulnerability to external domination. This susceptibility permeates all aspects of their social interactions, from friendships and familial relationships to professional engagements. The pattern of dependency is seldom confined to a single individual; rather, there exists an expectation that others will assume the role of decision-makers. Consequently, when numerous individuals exert control, it can provoke anxiety and diminish one's self-assuredness in making independent choices. This erosion of confidence breeds a reluctance to decide, culminating in a persona of indecision. Such indecisiveness can be a turn off to others, prompting them to withdraw from the relationship for their own emotional safeguarding. Indeed, few individuals are inclined to shoulder the full responsibility of another adult's well-being, given their own self-care needs. Although a controlling individual might not object, this dynamic significantly constricts the potential for cultivating profound and meaningful connections.

When We Are Doing the Controlling/"Fixing" Our Parents and Our Partners

Let's flip the script. What if we are the ones who end up controlling the older individuals in relationships? This may happen because we are our father's and mother's child, and we assume the responsibility to mend their ways or to become better parents to them. What if, in turn, we attempt to 'fix' others through forms of control?

A common instance where we feel compelled to "fix" our parents is when they divorce, and we are still young. We take on the burden of trying to mend the broken relationship. We believe that we are responsible for their separation, so we do all in our power to reconcile the marriage. It's more probable that the issue lies between your parents, not with you. Nonetheless, we instinctively react as if we are the cause. Another case is when our parents can no longer care for themselves, and we step in as their caretakers. This scenario is frequent, with aging parents' dependent on the support of their children.

They are your parents, which is entirely distinct from your associations with other individuals. It isn't your responsibility to mend or tend to others as though they require your aid. Our interactions with our parents often lead us to believe that we can extend these experiences to our relationships with others, anticipating that this will result in enduring and sustainable connections. Nonetheless, this approach causes us to lose sight of who people truly are, silencing their unique voices. It confines their identity and hinders our capacity to perceive them authentically, which one must remember, they are not your parents.

If we fail to grow beyond our parents' care, we essentially remain children wearing adult shoes. Our capacity for establishing personal limits becomes impaired, resulting in a loss of our own security and privacy. Confronting life's challenges single-handedly proves difficult when necessity demands it. We may find it arduous to interpret the emotions of others and to establish substantial, mature relationships. Our capacity to make autonomous decisions dwindles. We turn incapable of being present for others when they require our support.

It's time to let go of the duties imposed on us during our childhood. Let's move away from those who always expect us to care for them or shift responsibilities to someone else. Instead, let's agree to share responsibilities, with everyone willingly choosing to help.

FOCUS

THE PATH OF LEAST RESISTANCE IS JUST NOT WORTH IT

In our youth, we tend to go through life passively, reacting to events instead of shaping them. We let circumstances dictate our paths, falling into inertia and subjecting ourselves to the world's unpredictability. This complacency traps us in never-ending, unfulfilling cycles with the wrong people, often leaving no room for what we truly want. However, we have the power to change our lives with clarity and purpose, directing our intentions to guide our journeys toward our deepest goals.

A comprehensive study encompassing all age groups observed 6,000 participants over a period of 14 years. Throughout this duration, 569 individuals, constituting 9% of the participants, unfortunately passed away. A notable commonality among these individuals was their reported lower sense of purpose in life and fewer positive relationships compared to those who survived. The study found that, universally across all age groups, a greater sense of purpose in life was strongly associated with lower mortality rates. This finding is particularly intriguing given the general assumption that older individuals, who often associate their sense of purpose with career or structured daily activities, would exhibit higher mortality rates. The results underscore the significance of maintaining a sense of purpose and fostering strong relationships for individuals of all ages to enhance longevity and overall well-being.[32]

Sometimes, it feels like we're on a relentless search for love, and too often, it feels like we're searching in all the wrong places. Being young,

---

[32] P. L. Hill, N. A. Turiano. Purpose in Life as a Predictor of Mortality Across Adulthood. Psychological Science, 2014; DOI: 10.1177/0956797614531799

we stumbled into situations where we end up getting hurt without even knowing we're in danger. We often are treated less than we're worth, like just some kid, but the problem is, we get too caught up in our desperate need for love, for someone to stand by us, to provide that sense of belonging, and to offer their trust. Sometimes, we find ourselves in connections that have no real depth, no true purpose, and yet, we catch ourselves trying to convince our heart that this is what we really want. It usually starts off as something seemingly innocent until we take a hard look at our motivations and start to question the reasons behind our choices.

Where we look

Where we seek connections plays a crucial role in what we're hoping to find. If you're searching for a relationship on a hookup app, you're setting yourself up for disappointment, constantly let down by those who aren't on the same page. Similarly, spending every weekend in the same bar with the same group of friends can make you feel like you're making an effort, but in reality, it might just limit you. You might end up settling for someone familiar because you're not meeting new people.

Exposing ourselves to a diverse range of people increases our chances of finding the right match. It provides a feeling of progress and purpose. Once we achieve that, it's all about patience. Holding out and not settling, while keeping ourselves open, is the key to finding what we truly want. By being in the right places and targeting the right circles, we stay focused on our goal. We filter out those who don't meet our criteria and make room for the right person to enter our lives.

Cycles

Let's talk about the thrill of pursuit, shall we? It's funny how chasing after something, or someone, can give us such a buzz. Feels like a hit of dopamine is all it takes to get us hooked. And before you know it, you've gone from chasing one person to another, almost like collecting stories to tell rather than connections to cherish. But here's the thing - when the chase starts to turn into something real, something that might actually last, it freaks us out, doesn't it? I guess we're afraid of what it would mean to stop running and just be. Isn't that curious?

There are two cycles in particular that we find ourselves in because it feels good. One cycle being constantly hooking up with anyone that'll sleep with us. Perhaps because we are looking in the wrong place for what we want like a hookup app or simply entertaining predators without noticing they're preying on us. Another cycle is when we jump from relationship to relationship without being more selective or intentional with the person we choose to be in a relationship with. In both cycles, we love the admiration and validation we get from catching someone. We sometimes enjoy the act itself. Then, when it's over, the bliss we created in our minds go away and we feel used or feel like we're using someone else just so we can have that temporary bliss. We sometimes become numb and desensitized to that guilt and continue doing it with hopes to achieve a steady rate of bliss.

Sometimes we feel like we're forever running after something. It's like we're in this perpetual state of youth, not quite ready to grow up and move forward with someone special. We find ourselves caught in this endless game of pursuit, leaving a trail of heartache behind – sometimes it's theirs, sometimes it's ours. We just can't seem to break free from the thrill of the chase. We get addicted to the chase and can't seem to stop. We lose sight of what we seek as we become intoxicated with the dopamine rush during the peak moments of the pursuit. And then, when we pause for a moment, we can't help but feel puzzled and a little empty, wondering why there's still this nagging hole in our heart.

We sometimes can't figure out if it's them or us. We often think it is us and start attacking ourselves thinking we are failures. Thinking we are not capable. Yet we need to be in some sort of relationship all the time because if we aren't, we are not getting the dopamine rush. It hurts too much to be single and feel like a bigger failure.

We keep turning a blind eye to the gaping void inside us, just because we get pleasure on those fleeting highs. We lose care about the damage we're causing to ourselves or anyone else, so long as we get our quick fix of bliss. We're trapped in this endless cycle, incapable of breaking free to form real, lasting bonds. Too often, we're just spinning our wheels, unable to pull ourselves out of this mess and connect on a deeper level.

We then can take it to the next level and chase after those who don't want us – those who are already committed, or those who aren't looking for love, or even the ones who might just take advantage of our affection and leave us heartbroken. It's almost comfortable in a painful kind of way, reminiscent of the romances we may have observed when we were younger. There's this part of us that believes we can transform them, that we could be the reason their lives align with what we desire. Yet, once we've succeeded, our hearts races off in search of a new thrill.

Say for example we chase to date married couples, getting drawn into the orbit of their lives. We find ourselves captivated, wanting what they have. There's this feeling that if we're close enough to it, we're living it too. And yet, without all the strings attached. We long for that picture-perfect world but doubt we're up for the task, or even truly ready. So, we find ourselves chasing after these couples.

We ride out the heartache of being on the sidelines in their choices, all for the sake of capturing those peak moments with one or both of them. We're not their first priority, but we hang on, craving those fleeting instances of joy when we do manage to sneak into their time. We nearly fool ourselves into believing we're part of their world, but deep down, we know we're more like an occasional toy for them. We're put in a spot where we can either make peace with this part we play or pretend it's not happening. Whichever path we choose, it's a cycle that keeps coming back to sting us.

Cycles tend to instill feelings of depression, low self-worth, heightened anxiety, and stress within us. We trudge through myriads of low points solely for the sake of experiencing fleeting moments of elation that the cycle offers. The high points grant us a sense of validation, whereas the low points leave us feeling invalidated. In the favorable phases, everything appears effortless and devoid of stress, yet in the unfavorable times, we encounter pain and overwhelming stress. Such cycles can also give us the appearance of being younger than we actually are. They betray an immaturity, revealing that we are not prepared to manage our own emotional well-being or that of another. Afraid of responsibility sometimes. The root of the issue may lie in our external environment or within ourselves. Nonetheless, should we find ourselves in a cycle, it is imperative to extricate ourselves from it lest we remain eternally youthful in our disposition.

Let's suppose we interrupt this cycle and begin to follow others that align with our desires. You meet someone with whom you have a strong connection, only to discover they are similar to the type of person you were drawn to while in the cycle. This realization renders escaping the cycle an incredibly arduous task. It feels as though you never departed, despite your firm resolve to do so. This can lead to demotivation, dragging us back into the cycle, and instilling a sense of inability to achieve what we truly want and need.

For instance, you refrain from engaging in intimate encounters upon first meeting someone. Instead, you opt for a date to determine whether a substantial connection exists. Afterward, should a second meeting occur, it may lead to a sexual encounter. However, this individual, a prospective love interest, might depart without any further communication, prompting you to wonder why. Despite not having an immediate hookup, the situation seems just as fleeting, leaving you to question how it reverted to something so reminiscent of a casual encounter.

We find ourselves trapped within this cycle, struggling to escape. One might question, isn't this intended to be a self-help book? Although breaking an addiction requires considerable vulnerability, self-education, and commitment, overcoming it is indeed within the realm of possibility. Remember, you are not a boy or someones possession. It is crucial to delve deep into the reasons behind your strong attraction to particular types of individuals. What aspects render these situations so eerily familiar, and why do they consistently lead to pain? Consider whether the issue originates from within you or from others. Upon uncovering the significance of why this cycle persists within us, our next step is to steadfastly maintain our commitment to that revelation.

The more frequently we succumb to these casual interactions, the greater the toll on our self-esteem. With each instance in which we engage in a relationship that fails to meet our complete desires, it tears away at our very being. This cycle of events leaves us drained, breeding a reluctance within us to open up. We then find ourselves sealing off any potential opportunities, driven by a sense of futility. Alternatively, we might slip back into this repetitive pattern simply because we believe we deserve nothing more or because it seems like the sole source of our happiness.

Perhaps the reason lies in your reluctance to acknowledge your true desires. Alternatively, you may feel undeserving of such aspirations, given the extensive damage that has occurred. Or it may be that probing into the depths of the issues is too agonizing, leading you to superficially cover them with bandages. Regardless of the cause, there is no judgment. Succumbing to these situations is a common pitfall. Often, we don't even confess our failings because of the potential embarrassment. However, it is imperative to transform these adversities into sources of strength. Having endured what you have, you must harness that experience as ammunition to propel yourself forward.

Redirection

We first figure out where we are going. Then we redirect ourselves until we find a smooth path to travel on. We may run into a few unexpected turns that redirect us but with determination, steer back toward a smooth road.

For example, if your sole interest lies in engaging in casual relationships, this may be due to the extensive time commitments, which consequently hinders your ability to engage in or desire to shoulder the responsibilities of a more serious relationship. In such a scenario, it is crucial to actively pursue only casual encounters and to communicate unequivocally that this is your exclusive intention. It is essential to maintain transparency with both you and the other party involved. Should emotional attachments begin to develop, or if the situation takes an unforeseen direction, it is important not to pursue these developments. If casual relationships are indeed what you desire, you should steadfastly adhere.

Do not pursue casual relationships if you earnestly wish to be in a committed one. Initially, it transmits a mixed signal to your potential partner. Moreover, it reflects poorly on you when your initial impressions suggest that your only interest lies in something non-serious. This breeds distrust and prompts your counterpart to doubt whether your intentions align with your actions.

Suppose, for instance, you desire a monogamous relationship because you are weary of the superficiality inherent in casual relationships and crave something more meaningful. You long to devote yourself to a significant other, and you want them to reciprocate that commitment. You believe this is the route to experiencing complete love, unwavering support, a sense of belonging, and trust. Therefore, it is essential that you communicate clearly to your potential partner that you are seeking an exclusively monogamous relationship.

On the other hand, you should not pursue a monogamous relationship if, deep down, you prefer the freedom of casual dating. This can convey to the other person that you are not serious or prepared for a deep commitment. Additionally, should you align yourself with someone who does not desire a monogamous relationship, yet you continue to engage with them in an attempt to persuade them otherwise, you are likely setting both yourself and them up for failure, given the incompatibility of your respective paths.

Thinking someone will change is also the wrong place to be. It's a misguided starting point. Do we compromise and adapt for our loved ones? Certainly. At times, we are inclined to make these adjustments because we desire to evolve. Nevertheless, expecting someone to alter their ways to ensure your happiness is a precarious endeavor. Let's consider this from another angle.

Take, for instance, you feel a strong connection with someone who does not aspire for monogamy, whereas you do. You are faced with two choices: alter your own desires to reject monogamy or persuade the other person to embrace it. If you choose to change yourself, in doing so, you relinquish your personal desires and diminish your self-worth simply to please another. Conversely, if the other individual decides to change, is it feasible for them to genuinely commit to monogamy when it was not their original intent?

Consider the scenario where you desire to have a child, but the person you are dating does not. You face the decision of waiting to see if they will change their mind or seeking a different partner who shares your seriousness about starting a family. To make an informed choice, reflect on the significance of parenthood to you and weigh it against the value of your relationship with this individual. Over time, as your bond with them potentially deepens, you must confront whether you could accept a life without children in order to be with them. Alternatively, if you attempt to persuade them about the merits of having a child, consider the level of commitment they would bring to parenting.

I've always leaned into the idea that there's something quite magnetic about the way two seemingly mismatched souls can come together. There's a sort of charm in discovering the facets of someone who sees the world through a different lens. But when it boils down to the core of our desires, that's where we've got to meet eye to eye. Because at the heart of it, we're not talking about quirky traits or the way we spend our Saturday afternoons. It's crucial that our deep-seated hopes should dance to the same rhythm. If they don't, we might just find ourselves missing out on the richness that those other differences have to offer.

Creating Space

Have you ever found yourself surrounded by friends and acquaintances yet felt a little hollow inside? I'm talking about those barely-there bonds we maintain that feel alright on the surface, but deep down they don't quite hit the spot. It's not quite a cycle—it's more like an insatiable hunger, a hunger for more.

These shallow meet-and-greets can be fun for sure. Yet, trying to turn each of them into something profound is like trying to keep fifty best friends on speed dial—it's stretching the heart too thin, my friend. In that scattergun approach, we end up scattering pieces of ourselves, too. Instead of nurturing a few precious bonds, we're grazing the buffet of relationships without really tasting anything.

Sometimes, this whole scene feels like a standstill. Life rushes past us in a blur of moments and we're just... there, not moving, not taking part. Maybe, deep inside, we're hesitant to let our guard down, to let someone really see us, warts and all. Or perhaps we're standing at the crossroads of our destiny, frozen by the what ifs. Being vulnerable is scary, there's no doubt about it.

But remember this: standing still is a choice, too. If you're yearning for connections that matter, that truly resonate with your soul, it's time to observe what lies ahead. You're not going to halt the heavy-weight issues head-on or outrun them like racing a cyclist—but you can begin somewhere. Take those steps, one at a time, and you'll find the connections that lights up your journey becomes clear. It's about quality, not quantity.

When we find that sweet spot, the place where we just fit, something amazing happens—we blossom. It's like suddenly, we're not just drifting anymore; We're alive, fueled by purpose, and moving with intention. The chaos quiets down, and those uncertain corners of life start to clear up. We shake off those endless loops that used to keep us stuck, and step by step, we make choices that feel right to us. It's kind of wild; we catch a glimpse of ourselves and see someone who's growing up fast, someone who's got a bit of wisdom peeking through, even if we don't always feel it. And on those days when we're not quite there, just knowing there's a path ahead is enough to keep us from feeling lost, from being that young, unsure kid. It's like we've got a map in our hands, and we're on this journey.

UNLOCKING AUTHENTICITY

YOU ARE ONE BEAUTIFUL HUMAN BEING.

It's okay to not have all the answers, you know? To me, that just shows you're a person with your feet planted firmly in reality and authentic. There's no way we could grasp every single detail of this vast universe. Embracing our imperfections, letting them see the light of day – that takes guts. It's not something to be ashamed of, not in the slightest.

Sometimes, we hide parts of ourselves from others because we're scared to admit we don't have all the answers. Sometimes, it's because we're ashamed or worried about how others might see us. This leads to keeping secrets and makes it hard to be honest with ourselves and those around us. How can we build meaningful connections if we keep so much of ourselves hidden?

To break out of this shell, we need to be more genuine with ourselves and others. This means allowing ourselves to be vulnerable, sharing our secrets, and navigating situations even when we don't have all the answers, but still showing up as our best selves. It involves sharing our stories, working on being truthful and honest, and striving to reveal our true selves.

Being more authentic strengthens our relationships with others and with ourselves. It fuels our passions, gives us more energy for what we truly want, and boosts our mental health. It lays the foundation for greater confidence and a more fulfilling life. Let's dig into how to unlock our full authentic selves.

Secrecy vs. Privacy

Before we dive into unveiling the deepest parts of ourselves, let's take a moment to understand the delicate line between secrecy and privacy. Boundaries are essential, and it's here we decide what remains within us and what we share with the world.

Secrecy is the act of deliberately holding back something important, while privacy is about how much of our story we choose to tell. Both play a significant role in shaping our relationships. But we don't have to share our innermost thoughts with everyone we meet. When we yearn for closeness with someone special, we open up, revealing our secrets and maybe become more transparent. Conversely, when we wish to keep our distance, we hold our secrets tighter and share less.

Ultimately, the choice of whom we allow into our private world lies with us. Yet, with those we hold dear, secrecy has no place. Honesty should be the foundation, both for our own authenticity and for the trust we build with them.

Unlocking Your Secrets

A study involving over 600 adults examined the effects of secret-keeping on mental health and relationships. The research focused on the participants' preoccupation with their secrets, their satisfaction with their current relationships, the impact on emotional intimacy, and perceived levels of trust. The types of secrets included secret attractions, stigmas, infidelity, and addictions. These secrets were often kept for many years, sometimes throughout the entire course of the relationship, and were usually not disclosed to anyone.

The findings indicated that individuals who have a tendency to conceal secrets report poorer psychological health, less satisfying relationships, and a diminished sense of authenticity within their relationships. An initial hypothesis suggested that preoccupation with a secret might lead one to withdraw from their partner. However, the study found that those in less trusting, intimate, and satisfying relationships were more likely to be preoccupied with their secrets. This suggests that secrets are more likely a symptom of an unhealthy relationship rather than a cause of relationship decline.[33]

Understanding that secrets are a symptom of an unhealthy relationship rather than a cause of relationship decline, we can infer that strong relationships cannot be maintained if we keep things bottled up inside. The issue lies not with the other person, but with us. We are damaging ourselves and others with these secrets. We cannot establish trust or emotional intimacy if we are not authentic. Revealing our secrets, especially regarding attractions, stigmas, infidelity, and addictions, is incredibly difficult. But unlocking them is imperative if we are to become authentic and have meaningful, long-lasting relationships.

Think about that secret you keep tucked away in the deepest corners of your mind. Why do you keep it hidden? Are you trying to protect yourself, safeguard your reputation, or shield someone else's feelings? Is it constantly on your mind, weighing you down? Is it hurting your relationships or affecting your ability to form new ones? Secrets can bring about feelings of shame, guilt, and regret. They can undermine your satisfaction in relationships and chip away at your self-esteem. Keeping a secret might seem harmless, but it can be incredibly damaging.

Revealing your secret can lift this heavy burden from your shoulders and open the door to deeper connections with others. It can make you appear more courageous, more genuine, and perhaps more relatable. By sharing, we attract people who accept us for who we truly are, and we free ourselves from the stress and drain of keeping a painful secret. It also ages us. We become more mature and real.

If revealing your darkest secret just seems too much right now, let's build your authenticity with something less scary.

---

[33] Davis, C. G., & Tabri, N. (2023). The secrets that you keep: Secrets and relationship quality. Personal Relationships, 30(2), 620–635. https://doi.org/10.1111/pere.12472

Unlocking A Support Team

We understand by now that having support and a sense of belonging is crucial for our well-being. But how can we truly feel that sense of belonging if we don't open up and share parts of ourselves with others? And how can we expect support if we don't communicate what we need help with? Here's a simple exercise to help you get comfortable with sharing more about yourself. This can pave the way for the support and sense of belonging that empowers you to be your authentic self.

Imagine a moment when you felt utterly alone, even in a crowded room. A time when it seemed like no one else could understand what you were going through. Maybe it was something as small as being the only one wearing flip flops in a sea of dress shoes, or something deeply personal like being the only gay person in the room. Whatever it was, something that left a mark on you and has stayed with you ever since.

Got that moment in mind? Try sharing that experience with someone. Then, share it with someone else, and then another person. Open up, be vulnerable, and listen to what each of those people have to say.

No seriously, go try it.

Did you perceive them as understanding, prompting a desire within you to mend your issues? Did they offer consoling phrases? Did they tease you lightheartedly only to reassure you that your feelings are valid? Each of these is a positive reaction that likely enhanced your ease in disclosing genuine aspects of yourself. As you continue this practice, you will forge more profound connections and cultivate a more robust sense of identity.

If you've received negative responses, it would be wise to distance yourself from those individuals. Their reactions have revealed an indifference to your feelings and vulnerabilities, rather than offering comfort. They have demonstrated a lack of empathy toward you, for reasons unknown, suggesting that maintaining a safe distance or cutting ties entirely may be the best course of action.

You know, this straightforward exercise that's been a game-changer for me. It helps weed out the negative folks and brings to light those who genuinely have your back. Why should we waste our time with people who drag us down or don't stand by us? Honestly, I sometimes feel like I can be my own worst critic, no need for extra help in that department (just kidding, sort of). But seriously, imagine if your world was filled with only those who supported you. Sure, there will always be a few exceptions, but to be true to yourself, having as much positivity and support around you is key.

Think about all the people who you spend the most amount of energy with. Ask yourself these questions:

- Does this person fully accept me for who I am, and do I fully accept them for who they are?
- Can I be truthful, honest, and open with this person and are they able to do the same?
- Does this person treat me with respect, and do I treat them with respect?
- Can you be yourself around this person and can they be themselves around you?
- Does this person care for me and do I care for them?
- Do you enjoy spending time with them, and do they enjoy spending time with you?

If the answer to any of these questions is no, this could indicate that you are unable to be completely authentic, which might deplete your energy over time. You may discover that pretending or acting insincerely around someone is tiring. If they also seem dishonest or pretentious, it might discourage you from developing a deeper relationship with them. We engage with others through our emotions and require openness to establish meaningful connections. Not everyone in your life will answer yes to each question, but if there are negative responses, consider how much effort you're investing in that person. Give priority to individuals who meet all the criteria, and know that as life goes on, there will be new people to welcome and perhaps some to let go.

Some people are worth your investment. Your time, your energy, your money, your mental space. Others are liabilities. They don't align with your wants, needs, and priorities or perhaps not able to be your full authentic self. It is ok to not have certain people in your life. We can't physically and mentally maintain 30 best friends. A few that are worth your investment and deepening those connections make for a more real investment allowing you to have the highest self-esteem and confidence.

Embrace the power of being real with both you and those around you. It's the surest path to genuine self-assurance and authenticity. The thought of opening up can be terrifying, because judgment looms large. But when we keep our true selves locked away, we're nothing more than walking vaults of secrets. Sure, those secrets might feel like armor, guarding our privacy and giving us the illusion of control. Yet, they can be the very things that wrap us up in guilt, shame, and worry. We've outgrown that timid, scared child who used to hide from the world. With billions of souls out there, it's a journey to find that special circle of people who embrace us for everything we are, quirks and all.

When someone makes us feel like that child, we lose authenticity. We become someone they want us to become. We lose our own voice. We lose our experiences. We lose our value. Let's go over a situation when someone can make us feel like that child.

Overcome Seeming Dumb

When someone older admits to not knowing something, it feels like they're showing a humble and endearing side. On the flip side, when someone young claims they don't know something, it somehow comes off as if they're lacking and ignorant. So how does someone young express themselves when they don't know something?

Sometimes older people love to test a younger person's cultural references. Here's a few examples of what some people ask:

- Do you even know what a rotary phone is?
- Remember the minimum wage back in 1980?
- What did you think of the President Jimmy Carter?
- Remember the popular Mary Tyler Moore TV Show?
- Who wrote the book "Pride and Prejudice?"
- Who was the lead singer of Duran Duran?

There are many more questions, but it is likely that they are asked by someone who has lived through the times to which these references pertain, thus having more relevance to that person than to you. It is unreasonable to assume that you would know the answers without having experienced that era firsthand. We would need to deliberately research this particular subject, and it wouldn't occur to us to do so unless someone brings it up. So, how should you respond when you do not know the answer?

You are likely familiar with the saying, "Fake it until you make it?" Don't do that. Attempting to construct a façade with insufficient knowledge in front of an individual who is knowledgeable will only serve to highlight your lack of understanding and inexperience. Rather than pretending, adopt a different strategy: pose questions and express curiosity. Listen closely to the responses. Should an association to a topic within your realm of expertise emerge, steer the conversation towards your areas of proficiency and knowledge.

Admitting you don't know something and asking questions isn't a sign of immaturity. On the contrary, it's a mark of curiosity and maturity. This honesty also exudes a confidence and presence that others find impressive. They're struck by your willingness to admit you don't know everything and by your eagerness to learn more.

Remember, they tossed those questions out because they've got a clue or two already. Turn the tables and ask them questions like, "what has your experience been with this" or "I'm curious what made you think of that?" It's a subtle way of shifting the spotlight back, because chances are they're attempting to unnerve you, to make you feel like you're not quite up to their measure.

It's situations like these that make me question why do we play this game of one-upmanship? It's really about a need for control and a deep-seated insecurity. We feel driven to stand out, to show off some piece of information we believe others don't know – all in an effort to feel a bit more special, a little more important. Sometimes it's to make you feel even younger than you are to make them feel more powerful.

You are not young and dumb. You've walked through life gathering rich tales and unique strengths, the kind that often slip under the radar and overlooked by others. Don't get cornered into justifying your age by merely responding to their queries.

Unlocking Your Interests

What is unacceptable is feeling as though we lack compelling stories and distinctive capabilities. It is crucial to explore inward and acknowledge these qualities. All too often, we neglect to do this. This is the root of the difficulty we encounter in discussing our own lives, drafting a résumé, or writing an autobiography. We might underestimate the significance of our experiences, but we have all lived through noteworthy events, I assure you. What may seem trivial to you could hold greater importance to someone else who has not lived through it. By cultivating curiosity and sharing our discoveries, we can expand our horizons. It is in these moments that you can truly be yourself without fear of judgment.

One way to explore this is by asking your friends, family, and people closest to you what intrigues them the most about you. What experiences have you had that are so different from those of others and set you apart? Regarding work, ask others about memorable events that made working with you better and more significant. When did your work really allow you to excel? Also, share your thoughts with others. Tell them which of their experiences have made a lasting impression on you. These conversations help build our story and identify what specifically makes us exceptional.

Moreover, when we experience the compulsion to possess comprehensive knowledge and to impersonate an identity that is not truly ours, we compromise our authenticity. This leads to a transformation into an individual that an elder person may prefer. Embracing and revealing our genuine nature is not erroneous. Yet, we frequently retreat from manifesting our true characters out of fear of appearing youthful and lacking maturity. We refrain from embracing our authentic selves, preventing the world from recognizing who we truly are.

For instance, in my own life, I enjoy listening to rap music at a significant volume. However, I often keep this preference private due to the apprehension that others might judge me as juvenile or, even worse, that individuals with prejudiced views might perceive me as a threat. On one occasion, while at a bar with my colleagues, a rap song that I knew very well started playing. Unconsciously, I found myself silently reciting every word. One colleague observed this and expressed her surprise, remarking, "You're familiar with this song? It's one of my all-time favorites! I would listen to it constantly during my youth." This led to an engaging discussion about the historical context of some renowned rappers, which in turn fostered a stronger connection between us. She was a woman of advanced years, and I had harbored concerns about her judging my maturity level. Until that moment, I would never have associated her with a fondness for rap music. Yet, our mutual interest facilitated a situation where I could be my authentic self without pretense.

Consider reflecting on a personal interest of yours that remains hidden from others. It may be a particular genre of music that resonates with you. Or perhaps there are clothes in your closet that you cherish but never wear publicly because they speak to your individual taste. It might even be a hobby you engage in solely in the privacy of your own space. These unique preferences contribute to the essence of who you are. By sharing these aspects of yourself with others, you foster a more genuine version of yourself and shed the restrictive 'boy' persona. Succumbing to others' views on how your life should unfold, rather than embracing your true identity, should be avoided. You needn't permit anyone, regardless of their age, to judge your maturity based on your likes and dislikes. It's important to own your passions proudly. Often, you'll encounter people, including those older than yourself, who will either respect or identify with your enthusiasms. These are the individuals with whom we should cultivate closeness, enhancing the authenticity of our lives.

Honest vs. Truth

The best way to be fully authentic is to be fully honest with yourself and with others. This goes above just telling the truth. You can be honest without being truthful and you can be truthful without being honest. You can also be honest and truthful, but they are two completely different things. Let me explain.

Let's consider, for instance, that someone is cheating or being unfaithful to you. They assure you repeatedly that they are loyal and do not engage in infidelity. Nevertheless, despite their professed fidelity, they are indeed cheating, and you are aware of it. It's possible they believe they're being truthful and not betraying your trust; thus, in their mind, they are honest. However, in reality, they are not conveying the truth.

So, what is being unfaithful or cheating? "Cheating" is a word that seems to morph, taking on various shapes depending on who's defining it. To some, cheating is when your heart or desires wander into someone else's arms, even if it's just a look or a message. Others draw the line at physical intimacy, considering that the ultimate betrayal. But here's the real deal – we've got to sit down and spell out what faithfulness means to us, laying our cards on the table to see if we're playing the same game. It's the only way to ensure that we're not crossing invisible boundaries, unaware of the heartache brewing on the other side.

When someone chooses their words to seem upfront but keeps a slice of the whole truth hidden away, it can really throw us off balance. It's almost like they've managed to make us feel small without us even realizing it, preying on our trust and making our own convictions seem insignificant. It's easy to get swept up in what they're presenting as honesty, to the point where we start to question our own perspectives. We might find ourselves nodding along to their version of honesty, when deep down, we're craving the full, unfiltered truth.

What if this person is older than us and decides you don't get the whole picture? There's a shift in balance, right? Maybe they think we're not ready for it all, or that we're just not up to scratch to handle it. When they start calling the shots on what's big news and what's not without a second thought about how we feel or where we stand, it's like they've taken the reins. Before you know it, we're kind of riding along with their outlook on life, our own voice barely a whisper in the background. These seemingly innocent little white lies really can turn a dime on us quick.

Now how about being honest and truthful with us. It's crucial that we put ourselves first, not in a selfish way, but in a way that assures we are true to who we are, despite what others might say. Sometimes, we twist and turn our stories to fit into what others expect of us, but if we're not straight-up with ourselves, it's going to come back and haunt us. I know there have been times when I've bent the rules or stepped on some toes to grab something I wanted, even though it just didn't sit right in my gut. Even when we know we are not deserving of it. We've all been there, haven't we? At the end of the day, our own truth is what guides us to bed and wakes us up in the morning.

Isn't it a bit funny how opening up and being honest can sort of prompt others to do the same? It's like a small release valve. You know how you tell someone about something you feel, and you can almost see in their eyes that they've felt the same way, but they're just too scared to say it? I've always thought, why not be the one to break the ice? Why follow in someone else's footsteps when you can pave the way by embracing your own truth? That, in my eyes, is what separates just blending into the background from really standing out. Changes someone who is immature to someone who is mature.

Unlocking an Unstoppable Authentic Force

Once we start getting real with who we are—quirks, slip-ups, and all—that's when we kind of turn into these unstoppable forces. It's like we build up this superpower against whatever shade anyone might throw our way. There's something super liberating about just owning up to what we're not so great at, because then, what's someone gonna say that we haven't already faced head-on? It's so deeply important to hold on to your own truth and honesty. When someone tries to cast doubts, saying you can't do something, but deep down you know you're capable, it's all about clinging to that courage and steadfastly pursuing your dreams, without hesitation or fear. It doesn't allow the opportunity for someone else to take it away from you.

Being honest with ourselves also makes being lied to surprising. Realizing that someone has lied to us feels like a punch to the gut because, well, we never see it coming. We're playing the game straight, no tricks or falsehoods, and naively, we figure everyone else is too. That belief is built out of our own personal bubble and sometimes, honestly, we forget that not everyone thinks like us. However, when I catch myself lying—even if it's just the little white lies—I start to see shadows and deception everywhere I turn. It's weird like that, right? And yet, that heartfelt truthfulness, when we do show it and believe in its reflection in others, it forms these unbreakable trustworthy bonds, the ones that make everything seem so much more... real.

When we open up about our secrets, gather a supportive group around us, and are honest with ourselves and others, we become much better at dealing with situations where others might try to bring us down. This honesty helps us build stronger, deeper connections with both ourselves and those around us. It's important to distance ourselves from people with whom we can't be authentic or who can't be real with us. Embrace the uncertainty of not having all the answers, but also have the bravery to share your experiences and thoughts. Be straightforward and genuine and see if others respond in kind. By adopting these key principles, you begin to truly embrace who you are, moving past the fearful child who once hid from the world's judgment. This path frees you from the control of others who might try to direct your life, enabling you to shape your own destiny.

UNLEASHING CONFIDENCE

CONFIDENCE CAN GIVE OUR LIFE SOME CLARITY

I have learned over years of therapy and self-love how to confidently walk into a room and know I am showing everyone the best version of myself. How do we do this? We look deep into our feelings, express them, talk to others, move forward from past failures, and practice embracing our full selves to the world unapologetically. This is how we can unleash a powerful force of confidence within ourselves and to the world.

Too often we are told our opinions and feelings don't matter. We hide our thoughts at a young age because we're too afraid of others judging or criticizing us. Sometimes we just want to process things on our own without outside input so we can form our own feeling. But if we consistently bury our feelings, we stand the chance of succumbing to depression over time, escalating our stress levels, and finding ourselves incapable of opening up, which is necessary for forging profound and significant relationships and dialogues.

In "I Am Not Your Boy," unleashing your confidence is about more than just patting yourself on the back for your achievements. It's about delving deep to fortify the bedrock where true confidence can flourish. This journey demands that we not only celebrate our strengths but also confront our flaws, striving to become the individuals we genuinely aspire to be instead of conforming to societal expectations. We begin by mastering the confidence to express our feelings, advance to nurturing confidence in love, and ultimately cultivate an all-encompassing confidence that awakens the powerful force within us.

Expressing Our Feelings

The journey starts with a bit of soul-searching, trying to place a finger on the pulse of what's stirring those feelings up. To be honest, it's not something I can always untangle on my own—but recognizing the emotion and what's sparked it feels crucial. I mull over it, asking myself things like, "What can I do to ease this feeling?" or "Is there a way to see this differently?"

Advice:

It's important to bring others into the conversation. There's something about sharing feelings with others that can feel right. We all go through a rainbow of emotions and, more often than not, we keep it to ourselves. It's relatable and we all experience various feelings that we don't openly talk enough about.

When we engage in conversations about our feelings with others, it emphasizes our humanity; it grounds us in reality. Conversing about our feelings when we are young is especially daunting and vulnerable, as we often harbor the misconception that we lack sufficient justification for our sentiments. Yet, the truth is, we all possess these emotional experiences.

But be careful who you express your feelings to. Sometimes we pour our hearts out to those who aren't deserving of it and can steer us down the wrong path. Among us wander cyclical beings that do not offer the level of support we yearn for.

One cyclical creature to be weary of expressing your feelings to is an ex. For some reason, whenever I find myself sharing my feelings with them, it's like I'm thrown back into my teenage years. It makes me feel kind of tiny and vulnerable, as if I'm desperate for a nod of approval from someone who used to mean the world to me. And let's not forget, they're an ex for a good reason, right? Still, even in those shaky moments, there's a silver lining—we somehow muster the courage to face those old ghosts, and it makes me feel a sense of pride, like I'm growing, even when it's tough. We can find a strength of confidence when dealing with the demons of our past.

Expressing my feelings to an ex stops me from truly accepting that the relationship has ended. It's like I'm desperately seeking their affection again, regardless of who initiated the breakup.

If you experience the same vulnerability I do when opening up to an ex, which is tiny and vulnerable, it's wise to steer clear of it. Talk to others you are comfortable with. You know who dislikes your ex more than you? Your best friend. Your best friend more than likely seen all the turmoil you went through during that relationship and talking about past or current feelings with them gives you confidence to move forward from an old ghost. And if that ex should slide into my message box with a casual "what's up?" You bet I'm hitting back with a cool, crisp "my standards."

Even when you sever ties with someone, ensure you turn the experience to your advantage. It's an opportunity for growth. It is crucial to understand the reasons behind the disconnection, to identify areas for personal improvement, and to calibrate your expectations more accurately moving forward. Failure to reflect and adjust can lead to an unproductive cycle, allowing unsuitable individuals into your life repeatedly. Such oversight endangers your joy, peace of mind, and exposes you to unnecessary emotional pain. It's imperative to unpack these matters,

I say this from someone who created connection after connection constantly getting burned by disappointment and not reading the signs properly. It takes a lot of energy to stand up from that and find confidence to move forward from past failures. Especially when it happens so often. So how do we move forward confidently and what does that mean?

Advice:

Dig deep into what makes you emotional. Whatever you do, don't let yourself or anyone else bury your feelings. They are real and valuable to know in order to have deeper connections. Ground yourself in reality with what you're putting out there and what you want/deserve. Constantly realign yourself so you aren't running in the same cycle of hurt.

Don't Focus on Short Term

Most importantly, we should focus on who we want to be, not what is convenient or what we seemingly want for the moment. Let me explain.

Suppose you have a task that needs to be completed by day's end. Instead of addressing the task at hand, you choose to enjoy a glass of wine. This indulgence hinders your ability to work on the task. Should you attempt to work on it while sipping wine, the caliber of your output is likely to decline. Conversely, dedicating your attention to the task without the diversion of wine would increase the likelihood of an optimal result. However, succumbing entirely to the distraction of wine could result in the failure to finalize the task altogether.

You can equate the assignment with any long-term ambition you have. Whether it's maintaining a long-term relationship, making a career change, striving for sobriety, achieving something significant, losing weight, and so forth. Similarly, the glass of wine can symbolize any source of short-lived pleasure, such as making purchases, treating yourself to rich, fatty foods, casual romantic encounters, or substance use. The outcome remains consistent when you incorporate fleeting pleasures into long-term objectives.

Short-term happiness should never interfere with long-term happiness. Sometimes we need to sacrifice the short-term happiness in order to have the long-term happiness. Here are some examples of how this concept works in relationships.

Say you are looking for a long-term relationship with someone. You meet someone incredibly attractive to you and you want to entertain a connection with them to see if there is viability. Too often, we tell these people that we are open to whatever happens when deep down we want a long-term connection. We say things like, I'm open to whatever happens. I just want to go with the flow. I'm open to a hookup. The long-term happiness is the relationship, and the short-term is the hookups. You could have a relationship with the hookups, but would it be the strongest effort into finding a relationship? You could simply forgo the relationship and just hookup, but the relationship never comes. Or you could simply focus on only looking for a relationship.

You have demonstrated to that individual your lack of confidence in pursuing a long-term relationship, not only with them but with anyone. By failing to communicate your long-term goals, you have masked them behind a momentary form of pleasure. This behavior may originate from feelings of insecurity or indecisiveness. However, for the attainment of long-term happiness, it is essential to recognize and confront the barriers that hinder us. Additionally, you might be sabotaging your own chances. It is possible that this individual also desires a long-term relationship. You might have compromised the possibility from the outset.

Let us consider an alternative scenario. Suppose you are married and aim to be a dedicated partner. Your objective is to offer your spouse love, support, a sense of security, and trustworthiness. Yet, for some reason, you find yourself sexually dissatisfied within your marriage, perhaps it leads to acts of infidelity. Despite this, deep down, you wish to embody the ideal mate for your partner, though you find fleeting pleasure in sexual liaisons with others. Even with infidelity, you might still perceive yourself as a loyal spouse if you rationalize it with falsehoods. On the other hand, you could opt for disloyalty without upholding the pretense of fidelity, which contradicts your initial goal of being a dedicated partner offering love, support, a sense of security, and trustworthiness. Alternatively, you might decide to stay faithful to your spouse and fully embody the true nature of commitment in your marriage.

Let's take a moment to reflect. Even with infidelity, we still see ourselves as a loyal partner. The mind is incredibly powerful, capable of justifying almost anything, even if it causes pain to someone else. We might push aside the infidelity, replacing it with thoughts like, "I don't care about that other person. I only care about you. It was just physical."

Or "I still come home to you every night." These are ways we try to minimize the betrayal, cloaking it in excuses to make ourselves feel better. But deep down, we know it's causing hurt, and hurting someone we love is never what we intend. Yet, despite our vows and promises, we struggle to break free from the allure, and perhaps addiction of others.

Sometimes these short-term sources of happiness emerge from past traumas or experiences. There are instances when we seek solace in simple pleasures reminiscent of childhood, a time when life seemed less complicated. These fleeting moments of happiness are so genuine and comforting that they are hard to let go of. However, we must realize that this pursuit of immediate gratification can obscure the larger perspective. These pleasures are akin to candy: delightful in the moment but not conducive to growth. By clinging to these habits, we find ourselves not progressing but rather repeating the same familiar patterns of behavior.

How Do We Assertively Articulate Our Wishes and Achieve Our Long-Term Goals?

This endeavor begins with a precise comprehension of your overarching ambition. Upon pinpointing it, concede to any potential hindrances that may thwart your advancement. Be mindful that you will face occasional setbacks; nonetheless, remain assured in the fruition of your goals, provided you stay dedicated and avoid letting fleeting joys detract from your concentration.

How do we unleash the confidence that you'll have that long term goal? Well, you have to believe that you are deserving of it first. It starts with being authentic which means opening up to others, filtering out the garbage, being comfortable with others, breaking free from societal expectations being honest and truthful with yourself and others. We then use that authenticity to unleash a stronger confidence by not burying our feelings, learn from our past mistakes, and recognize the obstacles in the way. We start to feel deserving of it when we put in the work.

When we feel deserving of it, we start manifesting signs of it happening. Little by little, we start to see glimpses of our long term wants. Things start becoming clearer. It becomes addicting as we are attracting pieces of it until it becomes whole. We slowly become more confident that it'll happen as we persevere. We see ourselves growing and evolving from a child to full on adult to ourselves and others.

I've come to realize that, yeah, all this takes a good chunk of time and can wear you out. But you know, learning to hang in there is pretty amazing. It seems like we've forgotten how to just wait and see in our rush-rush world, always going for those instant fixes instead of playing the long game. Sure, slapping on a quick fix might seem like it's doing the trick, but it's not really getting to the heart of things, is it? Just remember, every drop of effort you put in—every bit of that grind—it's carving out a better you. As long as you don't lose that spark to pick yourself up and learn from each day, you're on the right path.

How Do We Exude Confidence in The World?

Here's a little exercise I often turn to when I need a confidence boost for the day. Before you get out of bed, think about your regular routine. Consider all the steps it takes for you to walk out the door, whether simple or complex. Plan to do everything you normally do as part of your routine but add this simple twist: avoid looking at the mirror entirely. Go through your entire morning routine without checking your reflection and try to keep this up for the rest of the day if you can. Trust in yourself and the efforts you've made to look presentable. Believe that you look great just the way you are.

The goal is to take a break from self-judgment. By not looking in the mirror, you eliminate personal biases and judgments, allowing you to face the world with less anxiety and more confidence. Forget about minor hair imperfections. Don't worry if your outfit isn't perfectly coordinated. This practice is a chance to nurture and share your natural confidence with the world around you.

Another little exercise to exude confidence: adopt a posture where your shoulders are pulled back and your chest is elevated. Keep your head high and positioned directly above your spine. Emulate a strong, purposeful stride, akin to striding down a fashion runway. Strive to elongate the appearance of your legs and maintain a direct path as you walk. Practice this posture for an entire day. Such a stance will instantaneously imbue you with a sense of significance and prominence in the world. It fosters an empowering sensation and the motivation that one is capable of overcoming any obstacle. Additionally, this posture aids in aligning the back, providing relief to those who suffer from back pain.

This exercise may require some practice. While running errands or engaging in your work, maintain complete focus on the task at hand. Avoid distractions from passersby or objects that may divert your attention. Perhaps don't look at your phone. Dedicate yourself fully to the completion of your necessary tasks. In doing so, you will observe that you're giving priority to each of the given tasks and will experience a sense of accomplishment upon its completion. Others will also take note of your focus and determination, perceiving a strong sense of confidence in your actions.

Remember I said before how you shouldn't "fake it until you make it?" Well, in these scenarios, do it. We can quickly alter our day simply by these actions changing the way we think. We can trick our minds to have so much confidence that we start believing we are confident humans. If we continuously believe that moving forward and it completely alters our future.

AVOIDANCE VS. PURSUIT

GO AFTER WHAT YOU WANT, NOT SETTLE FOR SOMETHING BECAUSE IT'S SIMPLY AVAILABLE.

Being young, we are sometimes expected to bend over backwards for someone older. We have to respect our elders. Maybe that was the case when we were young and developing and didn't know any better. But you know better now. You get to make the decisions on whether to stay in a situation or leave. You get to decide what needs adjusting. You get to decide what is negotiable or not negotiable. We sometimes fall into this trap that an older person needs to make that decision for us. Sometimes it's made without us knowing. You are not a toy that gets to be played with whenever someone else wants to.

We covered a lot of ground up until this point. In this chapter, without repeating much of the content we covered, I laid out situations of which to avoid and what to pursue specific to our unique situation as young gay men in the dating realm:

Avoid	Pursue
Social Experiments	Aligned Intent
Ageism	Commitments
The "Dream" Person or Fantasy	Relationships that go slow
	Boundaries

Avoid

Attachment theory, conceptualized by psychoanalyst John Bowlby, is foundational in understanding human development. In essence, this theory posits that children require a secure attachment bond to feel safe. When this need is unmet during childhood, they may exhibit behaviors such as crying or seeking their caregiver to alleviate the sense of threat. Persistent failure to meet this need can result in various social, emotional, and cognitive difficulties. Furthermore, attachment theory suggests that these early attachment experiences extend into adulthood, influencing our relationships. As adults, if our emotional needs are not fulfilled, we often feel distressed and may go to great lengths to address this imbalance.[34]

Have you felt any of these feelings?

- Find yourself struggling to keep a relationship together until theres nothing left of you?
- Tried so hard to make others happy that you end up hurting yourself in the process?
- Ignored the advice to walk away from others because your heart is too tangled up in the situation?
- Trying to "fix" others?

We often develop such a deep attachment to someone or something that the thought of letting go seems impossible, often due to unresolved needs from our past. Let's explore why we should avoid some of the situations listed in the table above:

---

[34] Flaherty SC, Sadler LS. A review of attachment theory in the context of adolescent parenting. J Pediatr Health Care. 2011 Mar-Apr;25(2):114-21. doi: 10.1016/j.pedhc.2010.02.005. Epub 2010 May 1. PMID: 21320683; PMCID: PMC3051370.

Social Experiments

A social experiment is when someone or you are using the other as an experiment for themselves. It's experimenting to see if they can handle something or if it's something they want. I've done this and it has been done to me. Testing each other and ourselves. Why is this a bad thing?

Social experiments are inherently self-centered. The experiment is not conducted with the intent to fortify the relationship. Rather, it's an exploration they happen to be conducting with you—or you with them.

It's seemingly innocent. Figuring out what you're capable of and wanting. But as a result, it's hurting the other person for one's own personal gain.

Remember, we all need love, support, sense of belonging, and trust. If all persons involved isn't getting it, it's time to reevaluate...

An example of a social experiment involves a person who is so dedicated to their regimen and lifestyle that the idea of giving it up for someone else seems insane. They enjoy the emotions that come with a relationship but fear that a relationship will disrupt their routine. This is common among older individuals who are set in their ways and refuse to make sacrifices or change their lives for someone younger. However, let's suppose this older person becomes so captivated by you that they are willing to step out of their comfort zone to be with you.

While it may appear to be reinforcement for the relationship, it's actually a social experiment for them - an experiment to determine if they can make such a sacrifice for another person. They have never before given up so much for someone else. Now you're faced with a decision: Are you comfortable with the idea that this social experiment isn't truly about you or your shared connection, but rather about them assessing whether they are capable of such actions, regardless of who the partner might be?

I was with Justin, a guy who had only dated women before. He had broken off an engagement and lived comfortably on his own for years. It was a big step for him to meet me and quickly fell for the idea of me—a man who reminded him of his ex-fiancé in many ways and encompassed the quintessential relationship. Things moved fast even though I tried to slow them down, and I got swept up in the excitement too. Justin had severe anxiety about stepping out of his comfort zone, so I often made things easier by visiting his place and arranging our time together.

He preferred seeing me when it suited him, and he didn't want to be a part of my life. If our plans inconvenienced him, his anxiety would spike, and he'd pull away. Justin was trying to see if he could overcome his comfort zone of solitude and fix a past relationship failure. But I wasn't his ex, and my lifestyle was different from his. I also lived an hour away. I went along with it because I really liked him and hoped it would make us closer. But in the end, he couldn't make sacrifices. As a result, I felt like he didn't love me enough to put in the effort. But in reality, his anxiety held him back from truly caring for anyone else.

Another example. Someone who has never been loyal. They meet you and feel like they can try to be loyal because you're this great person. While it's a compliment to you, it doesn't serve you anything to go along with it. It doesn't strengthen you, only themselves. In fact, it hurts you during the relationship while you're hoping for a potential payout. They can easy fall back into their comfort of never being loyal but they're trying it for you.

Do you remember the guy named Barry I mentioned earlier in the book? He couldn't commit to being monogamous but was so captivated by me that he tried hard to make it happen, knowing that it was what I wanted. Despite his efforts, he found himself addicted to apps and porn, unable to go a day without them. The idea of monogamy seemed appealing, but this habit plunged him back into a world of infidelity, which was something I simply could not accept.

If we truly recognize that we're part of a social experiment, it has to be explicitly stated and honestly embraced. Sometimes, people might go along with a situation not because they want to, but because they feel pressured by the circumstances. By doing so, they keep their relationship with you intact, though it may come at the expense of both their principles and yours.

It's better to steer clear of social experiments. Sometimes, they seem

promising and full of extra love, like someone's willing to move moun-
tains for you, and that's incredibly tempting. But usually, it ends up
with one person fully invested, dreaming of a future together, while the
other is just cautiously testing the waters, hesitant to dive in completely
because they're struggling with their own demons. That's when things
get complicated and personal. We start feeling disappointed because
the other person isn't living up to our expectations. We think they're
not showing up for us in the ways we need or want. But we need to remember, sometimes they have their own battles that they need to fight
on their own.

Ageism

Younger individuals in relationships with older people must work harder
to be taken seriously. Overdrinking at social events can harm our reputation, making us seem reckless. Appearing uninformed can lead to being
labeled naive and immature. Ageism based on our youthful looks and
actions can cause others to undervalue our abilities.

The older partner hasn't experienced life through your perspective.
Despite their different experiences, they are capable of empathizing
because they were young too but it's natural for both the younger and
older person in the relationship to have ageism tendencies. Having these
tendencies makes for situations like this as something to avoid.

True respect in a relationship comes when someone sees you for
who you are without prejudice. What matters most is being treated as
an equal, regardless of age. Equality means sharing burdens, understanding each other's feelings, and valuing each other. Older partners
might assume a leadership role due to their longer life experience, often
controlling the younger person, but they can learn from you too. Mutual
learning fosters genuine respect ensures everyone's voice is heard and
makes joint decision-making possible.

These relationships demand effort and constant improvement to
uphold equality. Assess if the relationship is worth pursuing based on
mutual willingness to work on it. Often, it's best to steer clear of these

situations since it's uncommon for both people not to fall into habitual ageism prejudices.

The Dream Person/Fantasy

Have you ever found yourself so head over heels for someone that your heart just refuses to even consider anyone else? You know, when you're utterly convinced you've found the one you've been dreaming of and you cling to the idea that it has to work out, come what may. Even if they are not good for us? I think we've all been there at least once – that space where we simply can't bear the thought of letting go, ignoring the little voice in our heads warning us to run the other way. It's that tug-of-war between the heart and the mind, isn't it? Should we follow our feelings and pursue with everything we've got, or listen to our common sense telling us to back off? The struggle is real.

We are attracted to a variety of people, and the notion of a singular soulmate seems sacrilegious. Consider that more suitable partners exist, partners you overlook due to your preoccupation with one person. This fixation blinds you to what you truly deserve, to the potential that the grass is greener elsewhere. Moreover, people regularly advise you to move on and seek another companion. However, what do they know? They are not privy to the depth of your emotions and the bond you share with this person. They are unaware of the sacrifices you are prepared to make and the efforts you're willing to exert.

Trust me, I have been there. I was so enamored by someone that the idea of anyone else was out of the question. My relationship with Justin ended with me being in an emotionally abusive situation. My relationship with Barry made me believe that no one could be monogamous. I kept thinking it would get better and that I could fix it. I couldn't let go, and that's exactly when it becomes most crucial to let go.

Sometimes, we need to experience someone else's emotions to truly understand the depth of our relationship. Even if others have warned us, we might not see or feel the warnings initially. It's crucial to learn these lessons on our own but still be aware of the risks. If we ignore warnings and proceed blindly, we risk being controlled, manipulated, or worse, unable to love again.

Walking away from someone you care about can feel like leaving love behind, but it's not. Love often surprises us when we least expect it. We're drawn to many people throughout life, with the idea of a soulmate being charming yet ever-changing. As we grow, so do our desires and needs, sparking connections with different people who touch our hearts uniquely. Each time love goes awry, we learn something valuable.

Pursuit

So far in this journey together, I hope you've taken some time to really look inward and figure out the kind of relationship you desire. Maybe you've set some personal boundaries and standards to help you identify what you don't want. I also hope you've found some tools to help you be more authentic and self-assured, giving you the confidence to go after what you truly want. Now, let's explore some scenarios where you can seize these opportunities.

Aligned Interests

This goes beyond just a simple interest that you or someone else might have. I'm a firm believer that opposites attract, and that it's perfectly okay if not all of our interests align. This difference encourages us to step outside our comfort zones, learn new things, and find balance in various aspects of life.

Aligning interests in this case means matching what you and the other person are both capable of and desire. Capability and desire need to go hand in hand here. For example, you might want monogamy but not be capable of it, or you might be capable of a long-term relationship but not actually want one.

When we meet people whose long-term interests align with ours, it's an opportunity worth exploring. Both of you have likely put effort into understanding what you're capable of and what you want. This is a chance to see if this mutual understanding can lead to a fulfilling relationship for both of you.

Commitments

Making commitments is basically about making choices. When we're committed to someone, it means we've decided, no matter who else crosses our path, that we want to explore things with this particular person. We've chosen to focus on this connection, regardless of who else might come along. It's truly special to find someone willing to make that decision for you.

If someone is prepared to commit to you, or you're ready to commit to them, it usually indicates that they've figured out what they need and want. Hopefully, it's based in reality and not just a fantasy. Deciding to commit to someone takes significant time and effort. It's much more than just the first date—it's about finding someone who is ready and capable of making a lasting decision.

Relationships That Go Slow

It takes time to really know someone. It means having countless face-to-face conversations or long phone calls, reading each other's body language, and figuring out if there's a spark. As you get to know each other, you have to be okay with being vulnerable, letting go of some privacy and secrecy. Reaching a point where you can be open and genuine with someone is like opening the doors to your most private spaces.

Taking it slow in dating is an opportunity you shouldn't miss. It shows that both of you are being careful about where to invest your time and energy. You're being intentional and mindful with your feelings. Going slow is actually a sign of emotional maturity. It's often mistaken for being hesitant or not wanting to commit, but it's quite the opposite. It's about making sure that every person you let into your life is worth your vulnerability. You don't have to be open with everyone, but the ones you do choose to open up should be those select few who truly deserve your time and energy.

Boundaries

Should you seek out or avoid those who set boundaries? Setting boundaries is important for yourself and others. Someone who sets boundaries is worth your time, and creating your own is a valuable goal. Ignoring the need to set boundaries should be approached with caution. Here's why:

Embracing our own needs and respecting others' is key to self-care, which involves setting healthy boundaries. These invisible lines of respect protect us from manipulation. Setting boundaries can be intimidating, often due to past experiences where our needs were ignored, making us feel insignificant. We might have witnessed a parent lose their identity in pleasing their partner, confusing the notion of love. This misunderstanding needs to be resolved to build true, meaningful relationships.

Not setting boundaries sends unintended signals. It suggests we don't know how to care for ourselves or lack inner strength, leading to unbalanced relationships. Decisions become overwhelming, we apologize for small errors, fear disappointing others, and sometimes overshare with strangers. This openness can lead to manipulation, making us feel undervalued or taken for granted, which impacts us deeply.

Here are some signs that may show you don't set healthy boundaries with yourself:

- Misplaced guilt: Agonizing over what people think of us and taking responsibility for things beyond our control or when we do nothing wrong
- Questioning respect: Feeling worthy of respect or catching ourselves in endless cycles trying to prove our worth, earning our way into the esteem of others one exhausting step at a time

- Unsure of our wants: Unable to articulate the things that bring us joy or what makes us run for the hills
- Self-Doubt: Unsure of the kind of people to allow into our lives. While trying to follow the rules or guidelines I place for myself, can I actually spell them out when the time comes?
- Inability to be vigilant: When our heart or energy is not into it, are we able to stand our ground and turn down an invitation with grace? Or do we cave and go along with situations that don't bring us joy because it's the path of least resistance?

There are various boundaries we might set for ourselves and others. Intellectual boundaries protect our curiosity, thoughts, and ideas. When we can't express ourselves without mockery, these boundaries should be stronger. Emotional boundaries determine with whom and how we share our feelings. For example, if overwhelmed, we might not want to discuss our emotions immediately and should express this politely. Sexual boundaries cover consent and privacy, such as refusing sexual advances or banning photographs. Material boundaries dictate how our possessions are treated and shared. Time boundaries help us choose how and with whom we spend our time.

To establish these boundaries and avoid manipulation, self-understanding is crucial. Take time alone to learn what defines you. Make decisions independently instead of relying on others, who might have biases. If you must seek advice, choose someone with no personal stakes.

Once you have a sense of who you are, list your likes and dislikes. Set rules and enforce them with people in your life. Prioritize your time and energy on those you want to be with and activities you enjoy. Take control of your destiny rather than leaving it in someone else's hands.

If you've ever sat back and realized that you've got this bubbling well of love, a circle of unwavering support, this cozy feeling of fitting in just right, and trust as steady as the old oak in your backyard – and all of it without leaning on someone else – you're exactly where you need to be. Sometimes, you don't have to throw your heart into the ring just because you think you should; sometimes, it's perfectly okay to step back and appreciate that you're complete on your own. Being young isn't a synonym for lacking; we can have a full, rich life with all our wishes checked off the list, with or without someone to call our own. It's not avoiding love, it's pursuing the best thing of all, yourself.

However, if you desire that love, support, a sense of belonging, and trust in others, you absolutely deserve it and can expect someone to give you that. It is ok to let someone give you these feelings and you to want to give those feelings back to someone. It's not dependency or filling a void inside us, it's chasing after what we want.

PART THREE

DISCOVERING WHAT YOU WANT?

YOUR WISH IS MY COMMAND.

Why is it so tough to really connect with someone these days?

I get this question a lot. When I think back, snagging a solid relationship was once on par with landing a decent job. College wasn't just about hitting the books; it was prime time to meet that special someone, too.

But now, things seem to have changed, haven't they?

How do you decide what you want?

Most folks truly don't have a clue about what they want. I can't help but notice that people often put less effort into choosing a partner than they do when deciding on a scented hand soap. But you're different—by making it this far into this book, you've already set yourself apart, taking strides toward your most ideal situation.

To help give you some clarity or direction, follow these steps to help you discover what you want.

1. Clear your mind

Take a moment to step back from your current reality. Reflect on your present situation and the thoughts that occupy your mind. Consider how you see yourself, both physically and emotionally. Acknowledge any biases or self-esteem challenges you might have. Think about the judgments you make about your surroundings. Maybe you feel your environment lacks opportunities or isn't filled with the right people. Perhaps you doubt your own attractiveness. Clear away all these judgments and biases, and picture yourself starting afresh, with a blank slate free of any judgement. These include, but not limited to the following:

- Location limitations
- Your looks
- Any kind of disability
- Any addictions (ex. sex, porn, attachments)
- A perceived lack of experience

2. List what you don't want

Reflect on all the hardships and disappointments you've experienced in past relationships. Recall how you felt when someone didn't commit, or when they failed to meet your needs and desires. Think about the things you've learned you don't want, whether from personal experience or perhaps from the insights in this book. Write down all those deal-breakers and non-negotiables—everything you now understand that doesn't align with your well-being. If you're struggling to come up with a list, here are a few ideas:

- Infidelity
- Situationships/side piece/hookups
- Little communication
- Lack of respect
- Misaligned priorities/wants

3. Imagine the world of endless possibility

Think about what the best situation for you that is can bring you the fundamental necessities; love, support, a sense of belonging, and trust. Don't think about exact personality or physical traits that are attractive to you yet. Only focus on what specific emotional needs you ultimately want in the most ideal world. Knowing you need all four to survive, ask yourself these questions:

- What is the ideal situation that gives you all four?
- Is there a perfect scenario that you've only fantasized about but never thought it could be in reach?
- Is it something you've always strived for, but it never came to fruition?

4. Add in non-negotiable traits

Think about the particular qualities that draw you to someone. What specific attributes do you find attractive in people? You don't need to get very detailed. Consider broad traits that appeal to you—whether it's someone with a great smile, fitness-oriented, classy, social, charismatic, or humorous. Avoid relying solely on stereotypical notions of attractiveness. Reflect on the aspects that are non-negotiable for your ideal partner.

For me, I'm particularly attracted to someone with nice teeth and a fit physique. It might sound vain, but I take pride in looking after myself and desire a partner who shares that same drive and motivation. Teeth are especially important to me. When I was 16, I used my first paycheck to buy a $200 electric toothbrush, and I work out every day. For me, it's not just about appearances—it's personal. I find that having a partner who also prioritizes self-care motivates me to maintain my health and fitness, making it a crucial factor when choosing a companion.

5. Broadcast it

Now that you have a clear idea of what you want and the type of person who can offer that to you, it's time to share it with others. Talk about it openly. This helps keep you accountable because people will check in and ask about your progress. It might feel discouraging to admit you haven't found the right person or that your search isn't going well, but remember, their questions come from a place of care. They are cheering you on because they want you to succeed. Additionally, if you don't put it out there, how will you ever attract it into your life? Others need to know what you're looking for so that the right people can come into your world.

6. Don't be distracted

Once you choose what you want, stick to it. Don't be distracted by shiny objects that are mere distractions. Be patient. Finding the right person that can give you what you want may take time but stand in your own conviction knowing it will happen as long as you stay focused and fight for it. Trust me, the world works in mysterious ways. Any short-term distractions will just slow the process down even further. I want you to win and sometimes it takes battling urges and others, but I know you will persevere.

ROOTING FOR YOU

YOU ARE NOT A BOY.

We've learned about the pitfalls that can ruin our long-term happiness. To have meaningful connections, it's important to recognize these pitfalls and stay focused on our long-term goals.

By being aware of these challenges, we give ourselves an advantage. Staying vigilant helps us avoid heartache and recognize when others are imposing their desires on us. Understanding this manipulation helps us dodge it effectively.

Apps often lure us into seeking satisfaction that's unreachable. Recognizing their influence lets us build healthier habits. Similarly, in situations that hurt our self-esteem, we must remember our worth and seek genuine love and respect.

Acknowledging that toxicity can dwell within us is crucial. This realization helps us become kinder and more considerate. By being self-aware, we're not just avoiding life's pitfalls; we're creating a better version of ourselves.

Remember, nobody's perfect all the time. We need to experience things firsthand to truly understand them. Like a therapist who won't give you all the answers, we sometimes need to figure out our path by facing our mistakes. When looking for a 'forever someone,' we might slip back into casual flings. These slips remind us why we're holding out for something real and lasting. It's all part of finding our own path to true, lasting love. Resisting immediate gratification can be tough, but the joy we find later is more fulfilling. Sometimes, we need a reminder of why we're avoiding quick fixes.

I wrote this book with a compassionate heart, fully aware of the challenges we, as young individuals, encounter in our personal lives, relationships, and careers. I have opened up and shared some of my deepest secrets to empower you, helping you recognize the strength you have within. You possess the power and determination to protect yourself from those who do not share your aspirations and dreams. Remember, no matter how kind or well-intentioned someone may seem, you have the wisdom to safeguard your heart and vulnerabilities from unworthy situations. I am confident that you have the capability and resolve not to fall into the seemingly innocent traps where others might sway or dominate your ambitions or desires. Protect yourself from these creeps. It's super important.

You know exactly what you want, and you damn well deserve to grab everything you need to crush it in this life. You've got to pour in the blood, sweat, and grit because with those, you're unstoppable. Don't ever let the noise of being 'too young' or 'inexperienced' BS cloud your vision. There's always a way up and out; you've just got to be relentless in your climb. We've got the sheer force to dominate, to become the ultimate versions of ourselves, to take on the world and leave our mark.

You are not a boy.

HELP

If you ever find yourself needing some extra support, don't hesitate to reach out to these organizations. They're here for us, and there's absolutely no reason to feel embarrassed or ashamed about seeking a little additional help.

National Youth Crisis Hotline
a 24-hour crisis line for any crisis from pregnancy to drugs to depression
(800) 448-4663

RAINN (Rape, Abuse & Incest National Network)
https://www.RAINN.org
Live chat online, or call (800) 656 - HOPE (4673)
24/7 Help
Nation's largest anti-sexual violence organization. RAINN creates and operates the National Sexual Assault Hotline. In partnership with more than 1,000 local sexual assault service providers across the country and operates the DoD Safe Helpline for the Department of Defense. RAINN also carries out programs to prevent sexual violence, help survivors, and ensure that perpetrators are brought to justice.

Love Is Respect (National Domestic Violence Hotline)
www.LoveIsRespect.org
Live chat online, text 'LOVE IS' to 22522, or call (866) 331-9474
24/7 Help
We offer confidential support for teens, young adults, and their loved ones seeking help, resources, or information related to healthy relationships and dating abuse in the US. Our advocates are trained on issues related to dating abuse and healthy relationships, as well as crisis

intervention. When you contact us, we'll listen to your situation, assess how you're feeling in the moment, and help you identify what next steps may be best for you. This might include brainstorming a safety plan together or identifying local resources to further support you, whether it's a service provider, legal resource, counselor, or survivor network to get in touch with.

SAMHSA (Substance Abuse and Mental Health Services Administration)
www.samhsa.gov
(800) 662 - HELP (4357)
24/7 Help
For individuals and family members facing mental and/or substance use disorders. This service provides referrals to local treatment facilities, support groups, and community-based organizations.

988 Lifeline (Suicide & Crisis Hotline)
www.988Lifeline.org
(988)
24/7 Help
The 988 Lifeline is a national network of local crisis centers that provides free and confidential emotional support to people in suicidal crisis or emotional distress in the United States. We're committed to improving crisis services and advancing suicide prevention by empowering individuals, advancing professional best practices, and building awareness.

The Lesbian, Gay, Bisexual, and Transgender (LGBT) National Help Center
www.LGBTHotline.org
LGBT National Youth Talkline (800) 246-7743
LGBT National Senior Hotline (888) 234-7243
LGBT National Coming Out Hotline (888) 688-5428
Also, Online Peer Support Chat and Weekly Youth Chatrooms
Provides vital peer support, community connections, and resource information through helplines and online chatrooms. Our services focus

on sexual orientation and/or gender identity and expression. We are the oldest and most comprehensive national organization of its type and scope in the United States, providing critically needed services regardless of age or geographic location. We help youth and adults with coming-out issues, safer-sex information, school bullying, family concerns, relationship problems, and a lot more. The people who turn to us for help often live in rural and conservative parts of the country and are frequently feeling severely isolated, closeted and in despair, with literally no one else safe to talk to.

SAA (Sexual Addicts Anonymous)
https://SAA-Recovery.org
Attend an SAA meeting near you
Our primary purpose is to stop our addictive sexual behavior and to help others recover from sexual addiction. Recovery was possible for most of us only when we accepted the fact that we were powerless over our addictive sexual behavior and that we were incapable of changing without help from outside ourselves. Many of us came to this realization when we started attending SAA meetings. In that setting we heard stories similar to ours and realized that recovery from our malady was possible. We learned through the SAA Fellowship that we were not hopelessly defective.

Project Know (American Addictions Center)
www.ProjectKnow.com
Text support online, or call (501) 273 - 3490
Aims to inform parents and family members of those struggling with addiction, as well as addicts and alcoholics themselves, about the options available for treating addiction. With a library of original content, as well as content from our sister site Child.net (launched 1998, now merged here), and a national directory of teen resources, addiction therapists, treatment centers, and sober living providers, we educate in simple language. While ProjectKnow.com is not meant to take the place of advice from medical professionals, who should always be consulted regarding

issues of substance abuse or potential behavioral health disorders, we do provide overviews and offer resources that can expedite the process of familiarizing yourself with addiction, drug and alcohol abuse, dependency, treatment and recovery topics and options.

RESULTS OF MY JOURNEY

I wrestled with the idea of sharing my personal journey in this book. Initially, I wanted to keep it strictly a self-help guide that allows you to chart your own path without any bias, focusing purely on objective insights from my experiences. But I decided to open up about my journey, not to sway you, but to equitably share my struggles in the hope that it might help clarify your own path and offer insights into why I made the choices I did.

I've faced significant challenges in forming strong, meaningful connections in my life. I found myself drifting from one relationship to another, from one hookup to the next, allowing others to influence what I thought I wanted, instead of making those choices for myself. Years of therapy and numerous experiences have brought me to the place I am today, shaping the way I now live my life.

What led me to choose what I want?

My desires changed often. I never stuck to one thing because I wanted to explore all my options. It was through experiencing things that I figured out what I truly wanted, but I wouldn't recommend that method. It brought me a lot of turmoil and slowed me down from achieving my goals. While those experiences helped clarify my desires, they came at a price. Looking back, I wish I had spent less time exploring and more time taking action.

When I first walked into my therapist's office, my life looked full and vibrant. I appeared happy, with a social calendar packed every single day of the week. My therapist was amazed at how I managed to keep up with so many people and maintain my energy. I believed I could have fifty best friends and that I was good at it.

Not only was I extremely social, but I was also having what I considered the best sex of my life. I felt liberated, moving from one person to another. I thought I was living the dream—well-liked, attractive, and adored. However, I was constantly seeking validation from others instead of figuring out what truly made me happy.

My therapist helped me see that I wasn't genuinely happy. I was addicted to the high of being liked and would do anything to gain approval, even if it meant having sex with someone. Over the years, I dismantled my entire life to pursue the goal of being in a long-term, committed, monogamous relationship. This, as you might have guessed, was all I could handle given my upbringing and past experiences, which hadn't provided a safe space for open relationships or fleeting love affairs.

Back in 2011, my HIV status led me to label myself strictly as gay. For over a decade, I immersed myself in the gay community, convinced that this was my true identity. However, as I embarked on my journey through therapy, I uncovered deeper layers of my attraction towards men—they were rooted in unresolved issues with my father. Seeking validation from older men filled a void that my father had never addressed.

Through therapy and my experiences with HIV, I eventually found the courage to embrace a new chapter in my life. I've started dating women, a choice that feels much more genuine and in line with what I've always desired, yet never believed I could attain. Initially, the acceptance of my HIV status within the gay community provided comfort, but now, with the realization that being undetectable means I cannot transmit the virus, I feel empowered to explore what truly resonates with me. This journey has opened doors, allowing me to pursue connections that reflect my authentic self.

My Past Experiences

I sat down and took a hard look at everyone in my life, evaluating how each person contributed to my happiness. I wanted only the people who lifted me up and genuinely supported me through anything. This led to some really tough breakups with friends and lovers.

I put a lot of energy into nurturing my friendships, often at the expense of those that truly mattered. Many of my connections were shallow, and in my effort to keep everyone happy, I let go of the deeper bonds I cherished. It became clear that if I wanted to cultivate my strongest relationships, I had to narrow my circle down to just a select few.

One relationship that stood out was with Justin, someone I've shared about earlier in this book. He was emotionally abusive, not out of malice, but because he was grappling with his own unresolved traumas and untreated anxiety. His lack of self-confidence often positioned him as the perpetual victim, trapping him in a cycle where he struggled to engage in a healthy relationship. I was drawn to him; my confidence seemed to both attract and irritate him. He would pull me in with charm, only to lash out in aggression.For a long time, I believed he was my soulmate, a notion I later came to realize was a fantasy. The idea of soulmates is an illusion, truthfully. We are drawn to different people as we traverse various stages of our lives. My feelings for Justin weren't about him at all, but rather a reflection of my own unresolved issues—an attraction rooted in my own struggles rather than in the reality of who he was.

Another significant breakups I faced was with two close friends, Barry and John. I had a loving relationship with Barry, who was married to John. They brought me happiness as I was emotionally close to both of them, and they validated my feelings. Barry initially love-bombed me, making me feel incredibly special. However, once I looked past my emotions, I realized what was really happening, which led to a lot of conflict.

Barry was addicted to sex, and I turned a blind eye to it more times than my heart could handle. He was married to a friend of mine, and they had an open, consensual marriage. But as time passed, I grew increasingly jealous. Barry tried to force me to accept their arrangement, and I thought I could convince myself to be okay with it because of the validation I received. Despite the pain, I kept trying hard to maintain the relationship, hoping I could handle it. But it wasn't aligning with my long-term desires, even though they made me sporadically happy.

People knew about their open relationship and saw me with them, leading to assumptions and a story in my community that I was accepting of such arrangements for myself. This narrative invited others in similar situations to approach me, assuming I was open to casual hookups. Deep down, I hated this perception, and it eroded my self-esteem. I ended up being seen as someone who was willing to sleep around for validation and attention.

I wanted to change this narrative, but I couldn't control what others thought or assumed about me. I could only control my actions and my truth. So, I made significant changes in my life, breaking off ties with people like Barry and John. I needed to prove to myself that I was worthy of something more meaningful, that I was capable of more, and that I could actually have what I wanted by changing my actions.

My Boundaries

Disconnecting from people who didn't give me what I needed wasn't enough. I had to make some tough commitments to myself. I realized I was addicted to sex, and it was taking over my life, preventing me from being fully present at work, present with the people I wanted to be around, and from focusing on my goals. I had to acknowledge the impact it was having on me and recognize it as an issue to begin the recovery process.

When it came to my sex life, I decided to only be intimate with those who had the potential to fulfill my needs. I began saying no to casual hookups, avoiding individuals with predatory intentions, and making it more challenging for people to engage with me sexually. I instituted a rule where I would go on three dates before considering sex. I also minimized texting with new acquaintances, encouraging more face-to-face interactions and phone calls. Additionally, I shifted towards wearing less revealing clothes, opting for longer, boxier outfits to make sure I wasn't sending the wrong signals. These steps helped me discern people's true intentions and protect myself from getting involved with the wrong kinds of individuals.

My therapist and I devised a plan for me to go 90 days without porn or using dating apps. The objective was to remove myself from the environment I was ingrained in and essentially rewire my brain to seek different, more constructive sources of dopamine. I combated my urges with workouts, socializing with strictly platonic friends, tackling house projects, and declining invitations to events where I might be tempted to seek validation through sex.

The first month was incredibly tough because I struggled to fully accept my addiction. Temptations were everywhere, and it was painful to resist. I slipped up initially, but my therapist helped me move past it without being overly self-critical. I'm hard on myself, but I was determined to break free from this addiction. The more sacrifices I made, the easier it became to stick to my goal. The more I enforced my boundaries and said no, the simpler it was to overcome the addiction.

Time has passed, and while I'm not perfect, I'm now able to recognize situations I need to avoid protecting myself and understand the potential impacts. This journey has brought me closer to the people I truly want in my life and boosted my productivity at work. I can focus better on my goals and feel more confident about myself. I've replaced my unhealthy dopamine rushes with productive and meaningful activities, giving me hope and validation that I'm moving closer to achieving what I've been longing for.

Perceptions of Me

There have been times when people found it hard to believe that I genuinely desire a monogamous, committed, long-term relationship because of my past mistakes and experiences. It felt as though, no matter what I did, I couldn't change their perspective. But I've realized that exhausting myself trying to convince others isn't the way forward. Despite any dis-connections or actions, I took to move closer to what I want, I often fell short of their expectations of me.

I've stopped making decisions based on what others expect from me and have found peace with my choices. These decisions are mine, and they reflect how I want to shape my life. While I don't judge anyone who chooses a different path, I had to determine for myself what love, support, a sense of belonging, and trust meant to me.

In making these choices, some people have labeled me as homopho-bic. I had to sit with that claim and genuinely reflect on it. The phrase "love is love," often used in support of LGBT rights, is a beautiful sen-timent. However, someone once told me, "Your body is yours. period," which deeply resonated with me. Your body is yours to choose what to do with, and that principle guides my beliefs. While I don't consider myself homophobic, I acknowledge that everyone has the right to make choices about their own bodies. My choices might not be for everyone, but they are dedicated to what works best for me.

ACKNOWLEDGEMENTS

This book has been meticulously shaped by my personal experiences in various relationships, including those with older individuals, the high expectations from my family, and the friendships I have formed with those significantly older than myself. The majority of my community comprises people who are older, and I wish to express my respect for the transformative impact they have had on me as an adult. Although in some instances their influence may have skewed negatively, I still value the positive facets of how these connections have shaped my identity. Absent these relationships, I may not have risen to the challenges that have shaped me into the confident adult I can declare I am today.

I extend a deep gratitude to my cherished friend Joe. We have fostered a close friendship for over twelve years, despite a thirty-five-year age gap. Our contrasting experiences have broadened my curiosity, compelling me to explore new perspectives and view life through a diverse lens. I am thankful for his unwavering support, his ability to maintain my curiosity, and his acceptance of my true self.

I would also like to extend my gratitude to my dearest friend, Erin. We have maintained our friendship since high school, and she has witnessed every transformation I have undergone. Erin's assertive voice and commanding presence have significantly influenced and molded my character. I am deeply grateful for her tremendous support, steadfast love, and constant presence throughout every challenge I've faced in life including the death of my father and my HIV diagnosis.

I owe a debt of gratitude to my mother, whose relentless drive to overcome substantial adversity serves as an unending source of inspiration. Her tenacity and refusal to compromise her authenticity leave me in awe. She remains my steadfast pillar of strength. Her enduring laughter and smile, even in the face of adversity, encourage me to greet each challenge with a smile and laughter of my own.

Acknowledgment is due to my father as well. Despite his passing and our weak relationship, with the help of my therapist, I've learned to derive insights that have enriched my life and reshaped my behavior. Our relationship, in both its highs and lows, has fostered continuous personal growth and the establishment of strong connections with others. Regrettably, he remained unaware of my various relationships—a fact I lament, as it may have strengthened our bond.

I also wish to thank all my former partners. Although our paths diverged, I am grateful for the joyous moments we shared. These encounters were integral to the formation of my identity and the achievements that followed. For all the laughter and joy, I acknowledge the goodness within each of you and hope for your happiness. Moreover, I apologize for any discomfort this book may cause, though you were forewarned.

To my therapist Todd, with whom I've met weekly for several years, I offer my enduring gratitude. Your guidance has enabled me to delve into self-exploration and has supported my growth. Though at times my experiences may have been challenging for you, your dedication to helping me through my struggles has been unwavering. Your steadfast support has granted me a clearer understanding of myself and fostered the deep relationships I now cherish.

I extend my appreciation to all the people I worked with and employers, especially to a former boss, Erica. Her consistent support and encouragement to embrace my true self daily have been invaluable. Her influence has emboldened me to confront societal norms and strengthened my voice in the workplace.

To my friends who continually offer encouragement and bring immense joy to my life: you consistently remind me that I am accompanied on my journey and never fail to elicit a smile from me. Your persistent presence inspires me to muster as much strength as possible and confront each day's challenges with tenacity. The joy you impart is immeasurable, and I am deeply grateful for your unwavering support, love, and the happiness you share.

Finally, to you, the reader, I extend my heartfelt thanks. The subject of this book and the adversity it encompasses mean a great deal to me. Sharing my experiences makes me vulnerable, yet I hope you can glean at least one insight to nurture your growth. I have observed the downfall of those who have failed to mature, stifling their own potential. By revealing much of my life in this book, I aim to support your journey. My concern for your future is sincere, and I hope that this book will guide you through life's occasional treacheries.

Printed in the United States
by Baker & Taylor Publisher Services